taste of home
BEST LOVED
cookies

PICTURED ABOVE: JUMBO CHOCOLATE CHIP COOKIES, PAGE 22
STAR COOKIES, PAGE 64 • SURPRISE CRINKLES, PAGE 46

OVER 200 cookie delights

GUARANTEED TO PLEASE!

From timeless chip-filled favorites to fancy shaped sensations, cookies are the perfect sweet treat. What other baked goodie stirs up heartwarming memories of sneaking a taste of the dough when Mom wasn't looking? With the delicious parade of more than 200 fresh-baked pleasures inside *Taste of Home Best Loved Cookies*, you'll find every type of cookie creation you've come to know and love as well as lip-smacking new delights, all guaranteed to earn a prized spot in your recipe box.

Featuring everything from classic favorites such as chocolate chip and chewy oatmeal raisin to sweet surprises like cream-filled sandwiches and melt-in-your mouth meringues, each bite-size wonder is a testament to just how much fun cookie-making can be. Seven mouthwatering chapters—Drop Cookies; Slice & Bake Cookies; Shaped Cookies; Cutout Cookies; Sandwich Cookies; Christmas Cookies; and Brownies and Bars—let you indulge your sweet tooth one blissful bite at a time.

You'll discover that cookies are not only the yummiest and easiest baked treats around, they are also ideal for any occasion. Bake up a batch of Apple Peanut Butter Cookies (p. 12) when you want a fun surprise to tuck in the kids' lunchboxes. Need a best-seller for the holiday bake sale? You can't go wrong with White Chocolate Cranberry Blondies (p. 103). If you're looking for the perfect finale to a special-occasion meal, you're sure to love Caramel Pecan Treasures (p. 38). And for a little excitement on a peacefully quiet afternoon, try your hand at Hazelnut-Espresso Sandwich Cookies (p. 69), perfect for dunking in a hot cup of joe.

In addition to all this fresh-baked goodness, our Cookies 101 section offers the basics for cookie-making success. Discover handy baking hints, tips for storing cookies and bars, ingredient substitutions, even advice on how to ship cookies when you want to send a special someone a sweet sentiment.

So spread a little love with these petite wonders guaranteed to warm hearts and bring big smiles. Thanks to everyday ingredients, step-by-step instructions and full-color photos, whipping up a fresh batch of cookies couldn't be easier!

Great gift! *Best Loved Cookies* makes a great gift for those who love baking. To order additional copies, specify item number 41736 and send $14.99 (plus $4.99 for shipping/processing for one book, $5.99 for two or more) to: Shop Taste of Home, Suite 445, P.O. Box 26820, Lehigh Valley, PA 18002-6820. To order by credit card, call toll-free 1-800/880-3012.

taste of home
BEST LOVED cookies

VICE PRESIDENT, EDITOR-IN-CHIEF: Catherine Cassidy

VICE PRESIDENT, EXECUTIVE EDITOR/BOOKS: Heidi Reuter Lloyd

CREATIVE DIRECTOR: Howard Greenberg

FOOD DIRECTOR: Diane Werner, RD

SENIOR EDITOR/BOOKS: Mark Hagen

EDITOR: Amy Glander

ASSOCIATE CREATIVE DIRECTOR: Edwin Robles, Jr.

ART DIRECTOR: Jessie Sharon

CONTENT PRODUCTION MANAGER: Julie Wagner

LAYOUT DESIGNER: Kathy Crawford

COPY CHIEF: Deb Warlaumont Mulvey

PROOFREADER: Linne Bruskewitz

RECIPE ASSET SYSTEM MANAGER: Coleen Martin

RECIPE TESTING AND EDITING: Taste of Home Test Kitchen

FOOD PHOTOGRAPHY: Taste of Home Photo Studio

ADMINISTRATIVE ASSISTANT: Barb Czysz

COVER PHOTOGRAPHER: Jim Wieland

COVER FOOD STYLIST: Sarah Thompson

COVER SET STYLIST: Melissa Haberman

NORTH AMERICAN CHIEF MARKETING OFFICER: Lisa Karpinski

VICE PRESIDENT/BOOK MARKETING: Dan Fink

CREATIVE DIRECTOR/CREATIVE MARKETING: Jim Palmen

THE READER'S DIGEST ASSOCIATION, INC. PRESIDENT AND CHIEF EXECUTIVE OFFICER: Robert E. Guth

EXECUTIVE VICE PRESIDENT, RDA, AND PRESIDENT, NORTH AMERICA: Dan Lagani

©2011 Reiman Media Group, LLC
5400 S. 60th St., Greendale, WI 53129
All rights reserved.

Taste of Home is a registered trademark of The Reader's Digest Association, Inc.

INTERNATIONAL STANDARD BOOK NUMBER
(10): 0-89821-889-6

INTERNATIONAL STANDARD BOOK NUMBER
(13): 978-0-89821-889-3

LIBRARY OF CONGRESS CONTROL NUMBER:
2011921301

Printed in U.S.A.
3 5 7 9 10 8 6 4 2

PICTURED ON BACK COVER:
Cherry Icebox Cookies (p. 26), Pastel Tea Cookies (p. 65), Chocolate Sandwich Cookies (p. 72) and Walnut Horn Cookies (p. 37).

For other Taste of Home books and products, visit ShopTasteofHome.com

on the cover

taste of home
BEST LOVED cookies
over 200 sweet sensations!

table of contents

PICTURED ABOVE: PUMPKIN SPICE COOKIES, PAGE 16
SLICE & BAKE ORANGE SPICE WAFERS, PAGE 26
DATE PINWHEELS, PAGE 34
CHOCOLATE LOVER'S DREAM COOKIES, PAGE 23

cookies 101

You can bake with confidence when you rely on these handy cookie-making tips guaranteed to produce delicious results every time!

before you begin

Read the entire recipe before you start, and check to be sure that you have all the ingredients called for in the recipe. Also make sure you understand the baking techniques.

Preheat the oven for 10 to 15 minutes before baking. Use an oven thermometer to verify the accuracy of your oven. If the set oven temperature and the oven thermometer do not agree, you'll need to adjust the oven temperature accordingly.

mixing it up

Prepare the ingredients before you start mixing. Let the butter soften, toast the coconut, chop the nuts, etc. Measure the ingredients correctly, using the proper technique and measuring utensils. Prepare the recipe according to directions.

Avoid overmixing the dough. If it's handled too much, the cookies will be tough. For even baking, always make cookies the same size and thickness.

When baking cookies, use heavy-gauge, dull aluminum baking sheets with one or two short sides. For brownies and bars, use dull aluminum baking pans or glass. It's best to use the size of pan called for in the recipe.

Use shortening or nonstick cooking spray to grease baking sheets or pans when a recipe instructs to do so. For easy removal, line the bottom of the pan with parchment paper and grease the paper.

Unless the recipe states otherwise, place cookies 2 to 3 in. apart on a cool baking sheet. For brownies and bars, spread the batter evenly in the pan. Otherwise they may bake unevenly.

while baking

Leave at least 2 in. around the baking sheet or pan and the oven walls for good heat circulation. For best results, bake only one sheet of cookies at a time. If you need to bake two sheets at once, switch the position of the baking sheets halfway through the baking time.

Use a kitchen timer to accurately time the recipe. Unless otherwise directed, let cookies cool for 1 minute on the baking sheet before removing to a wire rack. Cool baked goods on a wire rack to allow air to circulate. Cool completely before storing.

Let baking sheets cool before placing the next batch of cookie dough on it. Otherwise, the heat from the baking sheet will soften the dough and cause it to spread.

storing cookies & bars

Cookies tend to switch texture upon storing—soft cookies get hard and crisp cookies get soft. Here are some easy tips to keep these morsels at optimal freshness.

* Allow cookies, brownies and bars to cool completely before storing. Cut crisp bar cookies while they are still slightly warm. Allow icing on cookies to completely dry before storing.

* Store soft and crisp cookies in separate, airtight containers. If stored together, the moisture from the soft cookies will soften the crisp cookies and they will lose their crunchy texture.

* Flavors can also blend during storage, so don't store strong-flavored cookies with delicate-flavored cookies.

* Arrange cookies in a container with waxed paper between each layer.

* Store cookies in a cool, dry place. Cookies that are frosted with a cream cheese frosting should be covered and stored in the refrigerator.

* If crisp cookies become a little soft while in storage, crisp them up by heating in a 300° oven for 5 minutes.

* Cover a pan of uncut brownies or bars with foil—or put the pan in a large resealable plastic bag. If made with perishable ingredients, such as cream cheese, they should be stored, covered, in the refrigerator. Once the brownies or bars are cut, store them in an airtight container.

* For longer storage, freeze brownies or bars for up to 3 months.

* Wrap unfrosted cookies in plastic wrap, stack in an airtight container, seal and then freeze.

* Freeze a pan of uncut brownies or bars in an airtight container or resealable plastic bag. Or, wrap individual bars in plastic wrap and stack in an airtight container.

* Thaw wrapped cookies and bars at room temperature before frosting and serving.

shipping cookies

Here are some pointers to ensure that cookies arrive at their destination as delicious and attractive as when you baked them.

First, select cookies that are sturdy and will travel well such as drop cookies, slice and bake cookies, sandwich cookies, brownies and bars. Cutouts and other thin cookies might break or crumble during shipping. Cookies requiring refrigeration are a poor choice for shipping because they'll spoil.

Bake and completely cool the cookies just before packing and shipping, so they arrive as fresh as possible.

To help cookies stay fresh and intact, wrap them in bundles of two (for drop cookies,

place their bottoms together) with plastic wrap (see photo 1). Wrap brownies and bars individually. Pack the crisp and soft cookies in separate tins and pack any strong-flavored cookies, such as gingersnap, separate from mild-flavored cookies.

Line a tin or box with a few sheets of crumpled waxed paper or bubble wrap to cushion cookies. Tightly pack cookies to within 1 in.

of the top. Use crumpled waxed paper or bubble wrap to fill in any gaps between the cookies and sides of container and to cover tops of cookies (see photo 2). Close the box or tin.

Wrap cookie container in a cardboard box that is slightly larger and cushion with bubble wrap, crumpled paper or shipping peanuts. Seal box and label "Fragile and Perishable."

problem-solving pointers for cookies & bars

cookies spread too much

* Place cookies on a cool baking sheet.
* Replace part of the butter in the recipe with shortening.
* If using margarine, check label and make sure it contains 80% vegetable oil.

cookies don't spread enough

* Use all butter instead of shortening or margarine.
* Add 1 to 2 tablespoons of liquid such as milk or water.
* Let dough stand at room temperature before baking.

cookies are tough

* The dough was overhandled or over-mixed; use a light touch when mixing.
* Too much flour has been worked into the cookie dough.
* Add 1 or 2 tablespoons more of shortening or butter or sugar.

cookies are too brown

* Check the oven temperature with an oven thermometer.

* Use heavy-gauge, dull aluminum baking sheets. Dark baking sheets will cause the cookies to be overly brown.

cookies are too pale

* Check the oven temperature with an oven thermometer.
* Use heavy-gauge, dull aluminum baking sheets. Insulated baking sheets cause cookies to be pale in color.
* Use butter, not shortening or margarine.
* Substitute 1 to 2 tablespoons corn syrup for the sugar.

bars baked unevenly

* Spread batter evenly in pan.
* Check to make sure oven rack is level.

bars are overbaked

* Use pan size called for in recipe. Too large a pan will cause batter to be thin and dry.
* Check oven temperature with an oven thermometer.
* Check 5 minutes sooner than the recommended baking time.

bars are gummy

* Use pan size called for in the recipe. Too small a pan will cause batter to be thick and possibly gummy or cake-like.

bars are tough

* Stir in the dry ingredients with a wooden spoon. Overmixing will cause the bars to be tough.

crust is soggy

* Crust was not baked long enough before filling was placed on top.

crumb crust is too crumbly

* Cut in a little more butter so that the crust will stick together.

brownies crumble when they are cut

* Cool completely before cutting. Use a sawing motion when cutting. Warm the blade of the knife in hot water, then dry it and make a cut. Clean and rewarm the knife after each cut.

food equivalents

ITEM	EQUIVALENT
Butter *or* Margarine	1 pound = 2 cups; 4 sticks 1 stick = 8 tablespoons
Chocolate Chips	6 ounces = 1 cup
Cocoa, baking	1 pound = 4 cups
Coconut, flaked	14 ounces = 5-1/2 cups
Cream Cheese	8 ounces = 16 tablespoons
FLOUR: all-purpose cake whole wheat	 1 pound = about 3-1/2 cups 1 pound = about 4-1/2 cups 1 pound = about 3-3/4 cups
Frozen Whipped Topping	8 ounces = 3-1/2 cups
Graham Crackers	16 crackers = 1 cup crumbs
Honey	1 pound = 1-1/3 cups
Lemons	1 medium = 3 tablespoons juice; 2 teaspoons grated peel
Limes	1 medium = 2 tablespoons juice; 1-1/2 teaspoons grated peel
MARSHMALLOWS: large miniature	 1 cup = 7 to 9 marshmallows 1 cup = about 100 marshmallows
NUTS: almonds ground hazelnuts pecans walnuts	 1 pound = 3 cups halves, 4 cups slivered 3-3/4 ounces = 1 cup 1 pound = 3-1/2 cups whole 1 pound = 4-1/2 cups chopped 1 pound = 3-3/4 cups chopped
OATS: old-fashioned quick-cooking	 1 pound = 5 cups 1 pound = 5-1/2 cups
Oranges	1 medium = 1/3 to 1/2 cup juice; 4 teaspoons grated peel
Raisins	15 ounces = 2-1/2 cups
Shortening	1 pound = 2 cups
SUGAR: brown sugar confectioners' sugar granulated	 1 pound = 2-1/4 cups 1 pound = 4 cups 1 pound = 2-1/4 to 2-1/2 cups

ingredient substitutions

INGREDIENT	AMOUNT	SUBSTITUTION
Apple Pie Spice	1 teaspoon	1/2 teaspoon ground cinnamon + 1/4 teaspoon ground nutmeg, 1/8 teaspoon ground allspice and dash ground cloves *or* cardamom
Baking Powder	1 teaspoon	1/2 teaspoon cream of tartar + 1/4 teaspoon baking soda
Buttermilk	1 cup	1 tablespoon lemon juice *or* white vinegar + enough milk to measure 1 cup. Stir and let stand for 5 minutes before using. *Or* 1 cup plain yogurt.
Chocolate, semisweet	1 square (1 ounce)	3 tablespoons semisweet chocolate chips *or* 1 square (1 ounce) unsweetened chocolate + 1 tablespoon sugar
Chocolate, unsweetened	1 square (1 ounce)	3 tablespoons baking cocoa + 1 tablespoon shortening *or* canola oil
Corn Syrup, dark	1 cup	3/4 cup light corn syrup + 1/4 cup molasses
Corn Syrup, light	1 cup	1 cup sugar + 1/4 cup water
Cream, half-and-half	1 cup	1 tablespoon melted butter + enough whole milk to measure 1 cup
Egg	1 whole	2 egg whites *or* 2 egg yolks *or* 1/4 cup egg substitute
Flour, cake	1 cup	1 cup minus 2 tablespoons (7/8 cup) all-purpose flour
Flour, self-rising	1 cup	Place 1-1/2 teaspoons baking powder and 1/2 teaspoon salt in a measuring cup. Add all-purpose flour to measure 1 cup.
Honey	1 cup	1-1/4 cups sugar + 1/4 cup water
Lemon Juice	1 teaspoon	1 teaspoon cider vinegar
Lemon Peel	1 teaspoon	1/2 teaspoon lemon extract
Milk, whole	1 cup	1/2 cup evaporated milk + 1/2 cup water. *Or* 1 cup water + 1/3 cup nonfat dry milk powder
Molasses	1 cup	1 cup honey
Pumpkin Pie Spice	1 teaspoon	1/2 teaspoon ground cinnamon + 1/4 teaspoon ground ginger, 1/4 teaspoon ground allspice and 1/8 teaspoon ground nutmeg *or* cloves
Sour Cream	1 cup	1 cup plain yogurt
Sugar	1 cup	1 cup packed brown sugar *or* 2 cups sifted confectioners' sugar

drop cookies

Drop cookies are so much fun and so easy to make. Just mix, drop and bake for delicious treats the whole family will love!

PICTURED ABOVE: SUGAR 'N' SPICE COOKIES, PAGE 15 • DIPPED CHOCOLATE CHIP COOKIES, PAGE 11
CRANBERRY PECAN COOKIES, PAGE 15 • CHOCOLATE-PEANUT BUTTER COOKIES, PAGE 18

1/4 cup butter, softened
1/4 cup shortening
  1 cup sugar
1/2 cup packed brown sugar
  2 eggs
  1 teaspoon coconut extract
  1 teaspoon vanilla extract
  1 cup (8 ounces) sour cream
2-3/4 cups all-purpose flour
  1 teaspoon salt
1/2 teaspoon baking soda
  1 cup flaked coconut, toasted

FROSTING:

1/3 cup butter, cubed
  3 cups confectioners' sugar
  3 tablespoons evaporated milk
  1 teaspoon coconut extract
  1 teaspoon vanilla extract
  2 cups flaked coconut, toasted

- In a large bowl, cream the butter, shortening and sugars until light and fluffy. Beat in eggs and extracts. Stir in sour cream. Combine the flour, salt and baking soda; gradually add to creamed mixture and mix well. Fold in coconut.

- Drop dough by tablespoonfuls 2 in. apart onto lightly greased baking sheets. Bake at 375° for 8-10 minutes or until set. Remove to wire racks to cool.

- In a small heavy saucepan, cook butter over medium heat for 5-7 minutes or until golden brown. Pour into a small bowl; beat in the confectioners' sugar, milk and extracts.

- Frost cookies; dip in coconut. Let stand until completely dry. Store in an airtight container.

YIELD: ABOUT 5-1/2 DOZEN.

CHOCOLATE RASPBERRY COOKIES

chocolate raspberry cookies

PREP 15 min.
BAKE 10 min.

SHERRI CROTWELL • SHASTA LAKE, CALIFORNIA

The combination of raspberries and chocolate gives each bite of these cookies an elegant feel. Serve them for special occasions or any time you deserve a sweet treat.

  1 cup butter, softened
3/4 cup sugar
3/4 cup packed brown sugar
  2 eggs
3/4 cup semisweet chocolate chips, melted and cooled
1/2 cup raspberries, pureed
  3 cups all-purpose flour
3/4 teaspoon baking soda
3/4 teaspoon salt
  1 cup white baking chips

- In a large bowl, cream butter and sugars until light and fluffy. Add eggs, one at a time, beating well after each addition. Beat in melted chocolate and raspberries. Combine the flour, baking soda and salt; gradually add to the creamed mixture. Stir in white baking chips.

- Drop by teaspoonfuls 2 in. apart onto ungreased baking sheets. Bake at 375° for 10-12 minutes or until the edges begin to brown. Remove to wire racks to cool.

YIELD: 6 DOZEN.

coconut clouds

PREP 45 min.
BAKE 10 min. + cooling

DONNA SCOFIELD • YAKIMA, WASHINGTON

Coconut lovers will have extra reason to celebrate when they taste these cake-like sensations. The dreamy frosting and coconut topping make them a hit at holiday celebrations and other events.

COCONUT CLOUDS

APRICOT CREAM CHEESE DROPS

apricot cream cheese drops

PREP 20 min.
BAKE 10 min. + cooling

MELINDA LEONOWITZ
BIRDSBORO, PENNSYLVANIA

This treasured recipe is from a favorite aunt. Her soft, rich cookies have a yummy apricot flavor, but you could substitute strawberry, pineapple or raspberry preserves if you prefer.

- 1/2 cup butter, softened
- 1 package (3 ounces) cream cheese, softened
- 1/2 cup apricot preserves
- 1/4 cup packed brown sugar
- 1 tablespoon 2% milk
- 1-1/4 cups all-purpose flour
- 1-1/2 teaspoons baking powder
- 1-1/2 teaspoons ground cinnamon
- 1/4 teaspoon salt

FROSTING:

- 1 cup confectioners' sugar
- 1/4 cup apricot preserves
- 1 tablespoon butter, softened
- 1 to 2 teaspoons milk
Ground nuts *or* flaked coconut

• In a large bowl, beat the butter, cream cheese, apricot preserves, brown sugar and milk until blended. Combine the flour, baking powder, cinnamon and salt; gradually add to cream cheese mixture and mix well.

• Drop by teaspoonfuls onto ungreased baking sheets. Bake at 350° for 8-10 minutes or until lightly browned. Remove to wire racks to cool.

• For frosting, in a small bowl, combine the confectioners' sugar, apricot preserves, butter and enough milk to achieve desired consistency. Spread over cooled cookies. Sprinkle with nuts or coconut.

YIELD: 3 DOZEN.

cherry macaroons

PREP 20 min.
BAKE 10 min. + cooling

SHERMA TALBOT • SALT LAKE CITY, UTAH

I received this recipe along with its ingredients at my bridal shower. It was a fantastic gift because my husband and kids can't get enough of them!

- 1-1/3 cups shortening
- 1-1/2 cups sugar
- 2 eggs
- 1 teaspoon almond extract
- 3-1/2 cups all-purpose flour
- 2 teaspoons baking powder
- 2 teaspoons baking soda
- 1 teaspoon salt
- 1-1/2 cups flaked coconut
- 1 cup maraschino cherries, chopped

• In a large bowl, cream shortening and sugar until light and fluffy. Add eggs and extract; mix well. Combine the flour, baking powder, baking soda and salt; gradually add to creamed mixture. Stir in the coconut and cherries (dough will be very stiff).

• Drop by rounded teaspoonfuls 2 in. apart onto greased baking sheets. Bake at 375° for 10-12 minutes or until lightly browned. Cool on wire racks.

YIELD: ABOUT 6 DOZEN.

cranberry crisps

PREP 10 min.
BAKE 15 min. + cooling

SANDY FURCHES • LAKE CITY, FLORIDA

I developed this tasty recipe after sampling a similar cookie while traveling through North Carolina. These pretty crisps keep well in the freezer, so I always have some on hand for midday munching.

- 1 cup butter-flavored shortening
- 1 cup sugar
- 1 cup packed brown sugar
- 2 eggs
- 2 teaspoons vanilla extract
- 2-1/2 cups old-fashioned oats
- 2 cups all-purpose flour
- 1 teaspoon baking soda
- 1 teaspoon ground cinnamon
- 1/2 teaspoon salt
- 1/2 teaspoon baking powder
- 1-1/3 cups dried cranberries
- 1 cup coarsely chopped walnuts

• In a large bowl, cream shortening and sugars until light and fluffy. Add eggs, one at a time, beating well after each addition. Beat in vanilla. Combine the oats, flour, baking soda, cinnamon, salt and baking powder; gradually add to the creamed mixture and mix well. Stir in the cranberries and walnuts.

• Drop dough by tablespoonfuls 2 in. apart onto lightly greased baking sheets. Bake at 350° for 12-14 minutes or until lightly browned. Remove to wire racks to cool.

YIELD: 5 DOZEN.

chocolate marshmallow meltaways

PREP 20 min.
BAKE 10 min.

JOANNA SWARTLEY • HARRISONBURG, VIRGINIA

I loved these cookies when I was growing up. Kids are thrilled to find a marshmallow hidden under this cookie's cocoa frosting.

- 1/2 cup butter-flavored shortening
- 3/4 cup sugar
- 1 egg
- 1/4 cup 2% milk
- 1 teaspoon vanilla extract
- 1-3/4 cups all-purpose flour
- 1/2 cup baking cocoa
- 1/2 teaspoon salt
- 1/2 teaspoon baking soda
- 18 large marshmallows, halved

FROSTING:

- 3 tablespoons butter, softened
- 3 cups confectioners' sugar
- 3 tablespoons baking cocoa
- 1/8 teaspoon salt
- 4 to 6 tablespoons 2% milk

● In a large bowl, cream shortening and sugar until light and fluffy. Beat in the egg, milk and vanilla. Combine the flour, cocoa, salt and baking soda; gradually add to creamed mixture and mix well.

● Drop dough by tablespoonfuls 2 in. apart onto ungreased baking sheets. Bake at 350° for 8 minutes. Press a marshmallow half, cut side down, onto each cookie; bake 2 minutes longer. Remove to wire racks to cool.

● In a small bowl, beat the butter, confectioners' sugar, cocoa and salt until smooth. Add enough milk to achieve a spreading consistency. Frost cookies.

YIELD: 3 DOZEN.

dipped chocolate chip cookies

PREP 20 min.
BAKE 15 min. + cooling

JACKIE RUCKWARDT
COTTAGE GROVE, OREGON

These cookies are sure to impress anyone you serve them to. The white candy coating adds a wonderful flavor and makes them look so delicious.

- 1/2 cup butter, softened
- 1/2 cup sugar
- 1/2 cup packed brown sugar
- 1 egg
- 1 teaspoon vanilla extract
- 1-1/4 cups all-purpose flour
- 1/2 teaspoon baking soda
- 1/2 teaspoon baking powder
- 1/2 teaspoon salt

DIPPED CHOCOLATE CHIP COOKIES

- 1-1/3 cups flaked coconut
- 1/2 cup semisweet chocolate chips
- 1/4 cup milk chocolate chips
- 2-1/2 ounces white candy coating, optional

● In a large bowl, cream the butter and sugars. Add the egg, beating well. Beat in the vanilla. Combine the flour, baking soda, baking powder and salt; gradually add to the creamed mixture. Stir in the coconut and chips. Shape 3 tablespoonfuls of dough into a ball; repeat with remaining dough.

● Place 3 in. apart on ungreased baking sheets. Bake at 350° for 12-18 minutes or until lightly browned. Remove to wire racks to cool.

● In a microwave-safe bowl, melt candy coating if desired. Dip one end of cooled cookies in candy coating. Allow excess to drip off. Drizzle with additional melted chocolate if desired. Place on waxed paper; let stand until set.

YIELD: 1 DOZEN.

CHOCOLATE MARSHMALLOW MELTAWAYS

tip

cookie cubes

If you want an easy way to make all your cookies the same size, try portioning the dough into cubes . Simply line a baking pan with plastic wrap, pack the dough into the pan, cut it into squares and freeze it. Once it is frozen, pull up on the plastic wrap to remove the dough from the pan. Pull individual cubes apart and place onto cookie sheets to bake. This easy trick will also allow you to bake just half a batch and save the rest of the frozen cubes for another time.

frosted peanut cookies

PREP 20 min.
BAKE 10 min. + cooling

ALICIA SURMA • TACOMA, WASHINGTON

Oats, chopped peanuts and peanut butter frosting make this a nice change of pace from a traditional peanut butter cookie. After folks sample these, compliments and recipe requests always follow.

    1 cup butter, softened
1-1/2 cups packed brown sugar
    2 eggs
    1 teaspoon vanilla extract
    2 cups all-purpose flour
    2 teaspoons baking powder
    1 cup quick-cooking oats
    1 cup chopped salted peanuts

FROSTING:

1/2 cup peanut butter
  3 cups confectioners' sugar
1/3 cup milk

• In a large bowl, cream butter and brown sugar until light and fluffy. Beat in eggs and vanilla. Combine flour and baking powder; gradually add to creamed mixture and mix well. Stir in oats and peanuts.

• Drop by rounded teaspoonfuls 2 in. apart onto ungreased baking sheets. Bake at 350° for 10-12 minutes or until golden brown. Remove to wire racks to cool.

• In a large bowl, beat the frosting ingredients until smooth. Frost cookies.

YIELD: 5 DOZEN.

APPLE PEANUT BUTTER COOKIES

FROSTED PEANUT COOKIES

apple peanut butter cookies

PREP 20 min.
BAKE 10 min.

MARJORIE BENSON
NEW CASTLE, PENNSYLVANIA

These spiced peanut butter cookies are great for fall gatherings. They're crisp on the outside and soft on the inside.

1/2 cup shortening
1/2 cup chunky peanut butter
1/2 cup sugar
1/2 cup packed brown sugar
  1 egg
1/2 teaspoon vanilla extract
1-1/2 cups all-purpose flour
1/2 teaspoon baking soda
1/2 teaspoon salt
1/2 teaspoon ground cinnamon
1/2 cup grated peeled apple

• In a large bowl, cream the shortening, peanut butter and sugars until light and fluffy. Beat in egg and vanilla. Combine the dry ingredients; gradually add to creamed mixture and mix well. Stir in apple.

• Drop by rounded tablespoonfuls 2 in. apart onto greased baking sheets. Bake at 375° for 10-12 minutes or until golden brown. Cool for 5 minutes before removing to wire racks.

YIELD: ABOUT 2-1/2 DOZEN.

EDITOR'S NOTE: Reduced-fat or generic brands of peanut butter are not recommended for this recipe.

 tip

brown sugar

You can use either light brown sugar or dark brown sugar in this peanut butter cookie recipe. Both brown sugars are a mixture of sugar and molasses, with dark brown sugar containing more molasses than light. Light has a delicate flavor while dark has a stronger more intense flavor. They can be used interchangeably depending on your preference.

pistachio cranberry cookies

PREP 15 min.
BAKE 10 min.

ARLENE KROLL • VERO BEACH, FLORIDA

I came up with this recipe one year when looking for a treat that had a little red and green in it. The combination of cranberries and pistachios is delicious.

- 1/2 cup butter, softened
- 1/2 cup canola oil
- 1/2 cup sugar
- 1/2 cup packed brown sugar
- 1 egg
- 1 teaspoon vanilla extract
- 1-3/4 cups all-purpose flour
- 1/2 teaspoon salt
- 1/2 teaspoon baking powder
- 1/2 teaspoon baking soda
- 1 cup crisp rice cereal
- 1/2 cup old-fashioned oats
- 1/2 cup dried cranberries
- 1/2 cup chopped pistachios

- In a large bowl, cream the butter, oil and sugars until light and fluffy. Beat in egg and vanilla. Combine the flour, salt, baking powder and baking soda; gradually add to the creamed mixture and mix well. Stir in the cereal, oats, cranberries and pistachios.

- Drop by tablespoonfuls 2 in. apart onto ungreased baking sheets. Bake at 350° for 10-12 minutes or until lightly browned. Remove to wire racks to cool.

YIELD: 5 DOZEN.

chunky mocha cookies

PREP 15 min.
BAKE 10 min.

JANET SPARKS • SHIRLEY, INDIANA

My Home Economics Club has a cookie exchange every Christmas. These cookies, flavored with a hint of coffee, are always a big hit.

- 1 cup butter-flavored shortening
- 3/4 cup sugar
- 1/2 cup packed brown sugar
- 2 eggs
- 2 tablespoons milk
- 1 tablespoon instant coffee granules
- 1 teaspoon vanilla extract
- 2-1/3 cups all-purpose flour
- 2 tablespoons baking cocoa
- 1 teaspoon baking soda
- 1/2 teaspoon salt
- 1 cup chopped pecans
- 1 cup (6 ounces) semisweet chocolate chips
- 3/4 cup raisins
- 3/4 cup flaked coconut

- In a large bowl, cream shortening and sugars until light and fluffy. Beat in eggs. Beat in the milk, coffee granules and vanilla. Combine the flour, cocoa, baking soda and salt; add to the creamed mixture and mix well. Fold in the pecans, chips, raisins and coconut.

- Drop by rounded tablespoonfuls 2 in. apart onto ungreased baking sheets. Bake at 375° for 10-12 minutes or until golden brown.

YIELD: ABOUT 6 DOZEN.

dipped macaroons

PREP 20 min.
BAKE 15 min. + standing

LILLIAN MCDIVITT • ROCHESTER HILLS, MICHIGAN

I always get compliments from my kids, grandkids and great-grandkids on these elegant bites. Dipping macaroons in chocolate makes them uncommonly good!

- 2-2/3 cups flaked coconut
- 2/3 cup sugar
- 6 tablespoons all-purpose flour
- 1/4 teaspoon salt
- 4 egg whites
- 1/2 to 1 teaspoon almond extract
- 2 cups milk chocolate chips
- 1 tablespoon shortening

- In a large bowl, combine the coconut, sugar, flour and salt. Stir in egg whites and almond extract; mix well. Drop by rounded teaspoonfuls onto greased baking sheets. Bake at 325° for 15-20 minutes or until golden brown. Cool for 2 minutes before removing to wire racks.

- In a microwave, melt chips and shortening; stir until smooth. Dip half of each cookie in mixture; allow excess to drip off. Place on waxed paper; let stand until set.

YIELD: ABOUT 3 DOZEN.

PISTACHIO CRANBERRY COOKIES

SOFT ORANGE MOLASSES DROPS

butterscotch peanut treats

PREP 30 min.

BERNICE MARTINONI • PETALUMA, CALIFORNIA

I use pudding mix to stir up these sweet, crunchy no-bake delights. If you like butterscotch, you will love these delicious goodies.

- 1/2 cup corn syrup
- 1/3 cup butter, cubed
- 1 package (3.5 ounces) cook-and-serve butterscotch pudding mix
- 4 cups cornflakes
- 1 cup coarsely chopped dry roasted peanuts

- In a large heavy saucepan, cook and stir the corn syrup and butter until butter is melted. Stir in pudding mix until blended. Cook and stir until mixture comes to a boil. Cook and stir 1 minute longer.

- Remove from heat. Cool for 1 minute, stirring several times. Stir in cornflakes and peanuts until evenly coated.

- Drop the dough by rounded tablespoonfuls onto waxed paper-lined baking sheets; cool.

YIELD: ABOUT 2-1/2 DOZEN.

polka-dot macaroons

PREP 15 min.
BAKE 10 min.

JANICE LASS • DORR, MICHIGAN

These chewy macaroons are really easy to mix up in a hurry, and they're a favorite with both adults and kids. I've been baking for 35 years and believe me, these never last long!

- 5 cups flaked coconut
- 1 can (14 ounces) sweetened condensed milk
- 1/2 cup all-purpose flour
- 1-1/2 cups M&M's miniature baking bits

- In a large bowl, combine the coconut, milk and flour. Stir in baking bits.

- Drop by rounded tablespoonfuls 2 in. apart onto baking sheets coated with cooking spray. Bake at 350° for 8-10 minutes or until edges are lightly browned. Remove to wire racks.

YIELD: ABOUT 4-1/2 DOZEN.

soft orange molasses drops

PREP 20 min.
BAKE 10 min. + cooling

BEVERLY STEINER • MT. CORY, OHIO

Orange juice and peel add a slight citrus twist to ordinary molasses cookies. I've also stirred in chopped nuts, raisins, prunes and apricots.

- 1/2 cup butter, softened
- 1/2 cup sugar
- 1 egg
- 2-1/2 cups all-purpose flour
- 1 teaspoon baking soda
- 1 teaspoon ground ginger
- 1/2 teaspoon *each* ground cinnamon, cloves and nutmeg
- 1/2 cup molasses
- 1/4 cup orange juice
- 2 teaspoons grated orange peel

GLAZE:
- 1 cup confectioners' sugar
- 1 to 2 tablespoons orange juice

- In a large bowl, cream butter and sugar until light and fluffy. Beat in egg. Combine flour, baking soda and spices. Combine molasses, orange juice and peel. Add dry ingredients to the creamed mixture alternately with molasses mixture, beating well after each addition.

- Drop dough by tablespoonfuls 2 in. apart onto greased baking sheets. Bake at 375° for 10-12 minutes or until edges are set. Remove to wire racks to cool completely.

- For the glaze, combine confectioners' sugar and enough orange juice to achieve desired consistency. Spread over cooled cookies.

YIELD: 5 DOZEN.

cranberry pecan cookies

PREP 10 min.
BAKE 10 min.

LOUISE HAWKINS • LUBBOCK, TEXAS

These are so tasty and simple to prepare! Each delightful little bite is loaded with cranberries, nuts and vanilla, giving them the taste of a treat that's been slaved over.

- 1 tube (16-1/2 ounces) refrigerated sugar cookie dough, softened
- 1 cup chopped pecans
- 2/3 cup white baking chips
- 2/3 cup dried cranberries
- 1 teaspoon vanilla extract

- In a large bowl, combine the cookie dough, pecans, chips, cranberries and vanilla. Drop by tablespoonfuls 2 in. apart onto ungreased baking sheets.

- Bake at 350° for 10-12 minutes or until lightly browned. Cool for 2 minutes before removing from pans to wire racks. Store cookies in an airtight container.

YIELD: ABOUT 3-1/2 DOZEN.

no-bake choco-nut chews

PREP 20 min. + cooling

ANDREA SU • BINGHAMTON, NEW YORK

We have a hard time keeping these yummy chews in our house for long, so it's good that they're quick and easy to make!

- 2 ounces unsweetened chocolate
- 2 cups sugar
- 1/2 cup 2% milk
- 1/2 cup butter, cubed
- 1/2 cup peanut butter
- 1 teaspoon vanilla extract
- 4 cups quick-cooking oats
- 1/3 cup chopped walnuts

- In a large saucepan, bring chocolate, sugar and milk to a boil; boil for 1 minute, stirring constantly. Remove from the heat; add butter, peanut butter, vanilla, oats and nuts.

- Drop by tablespoonfuls onto waxed paper. Allow to harden, about 20 minutes, before peeling off paper.

YIELD: 3-4 DOZEN.

SUGAR 'N' SPICE COOKIES

sugar 'n' spice cookies

PREP 20 min.
BAKE 10 min. + cooling

DOTTIE LAPIERRE • WOBURN, MASSACHUSETTS

These sweet and spicy cookies are a special snack. The lemon frosting is the crowning touch.

- 3/4 cup shortening
- 1 cup sugar
- 1 egg
- 1/4 cup molasses
- 2 cups all-purpose flour
- 1-1/2 teaspoons ground ginger
- 1 teaspoon baking soda
- 1 teaspoon ground cinnamon
- 3/4 teaspoon ground cloves
- 1/2 teaspoon salt

LEMON FROSTING:
- 2 cups confectioners' sugar
- 3 tablespoons butter, softened
- 1 teaspoon grated lemon peel
- 3 to 4 tablespoons lemon juice

- In a bowl, cream shortening and sugar until light and fluffy. Add egg; mix well. Beat in molasses. Combine dry ingredients; add to creamed mixture and mix well.

- Drop dough by rounded teaspoonfuls onto greased baking sheets. Bake at 350° for 8-10 minutes. Remove to wire racks; cool.

- For the frosting, cream the confectioners' sugar, butter and peel in a bowl. Gradually add lemon juice, beating until frosting achieves desired spreading consistency. Frost cookies.

YIELD: ABOUT 4-1/2 DOZEN.

CRANBERRY PECAN COOKIES

PUMPKIN SPICE COOKIES

pumpkin spice cookies

PREP 20 min.
BAKE 10 min. + cooling

BEV MARTIN • HARDIN, MONTANA

These soft bites are almost like little pieces of cake. With chopped pecans sprinkled over a confectioners' sugar frosting, they're a pretty addition to a dessert table.

- 1 package (8 ounces) cream cheese, softened
- 1-1/2 cups packed brown sugar
- 1/2 cup sugar
- 2 eggs
- 1 cup canned pumpkin
- 1 teaspoon vanilla extract
- 3-1/2 cups all-purpose flour
- 1 to 1-1/2 teaspoons pumpkin pie spice
- 1 teaspoon baking soda
- 1 teaspoon salt
- 1/2 teaspoon baking powder

FROSTING:
- 2 cups confectioners' sugar
- 1/4 cup butter, melted
- 1 teaspoon vanilla extract
- 2 to 3 tablespoons boiling water
- 2 cups chopped pecans

- In a large bowl, beat cream cheese and sugars until smooth. Add eggs, one at a time, beating well after each addition. Beat in pumpkin and vanilla. Combine the dry ingredients; gradually add to pumpkin mixture and mix well.
- Drop by rounded teaspoonfuls 2 in. apart onto ungreased baking sheets. Bake at 350°

for 10-12 minutes or until golden brown. Remove to wire racks to cool.
- For the frosting, in a small bowl, combine the confectioners' sugar, butter, vanilla and enough water to achieve frosting consistency. Frost cookies; sprinkle with pecans.

YIELD: 7 DOZEN.

oatmeal cookies

PREP 15 min.
BAKE 10 min.

LAURA LETOBAR • LIVONIA, MICHIGAN

These lightly sweet cookies not only taste fantastic, but they are also low in fat.

- 3 cups quick-cooking oats
- 2/3 cup all-purpose flour
- 2/3 cup sugar
- 1/3 cup packed brown sugar
- 1 teaspoon baking powder
- 1/4 teaspoon salt
- 1/2 cup egg substitute
- 1/3 cup light corn syrup
- 1 teaspoon vanilla extract

- In a large bowl, combine the oats, flour, sugars, baking powder and salt. Add the egg substitute, corn syrup and vanilla; mix well.
- Drop by rounded teaspoonfuls onto baking sheets coated with cooking spray. Bake at 350° for 10-12 minutes. Remove to wire racks.

YIELD: 2 DOZEN.

almond sandies

PREP 20 min.
BAKE 25 min.

JOYCE PIERCE • CALEDONIA, MICHIGAN

Buttery, rich and delicious, these sandies are my husband's favorite cookie. They are very popular wherever I take them.

- 1 cup butter, softened
- 1 cup sugar
- 1 teaspoon almond extract
- 1-3/4 cups all-purpose flour
- 1/2 teaspoon baking soda
- 1/4 teaspoon baking powder
- 1/4 teaspoon salt
- 1/2 cup slivered almonds

- In a bowl, cream butter and sugar. Add the extract; mix well.

- Combine the flour, baking soda, baking powder and salt; gradually add to creamed mixture. Fold in almonds.
- Drop dough by rounded teaspoonfuls onto ungreased baking sheets. Bake at 300° for 22-24 minutes or until edges are lightly browned. Cool cookies for 1-2 minutes before removing to wire racks.

YIELD: ABOUT 4 DOZEN.

soft lemonade cookies

PREP 10 min.
BAKE 10 min. + cooling

MARGO NEUHAUSER • BAKERSFIELD, CALIFORNIA

These lovely lemon cookies are so moist, you won't be able to stop eating them! Frozen lemonade concentrate is the surprise ingredient.

- 1 cup butter, softened
- 1 cup sugar
- 2 eggs
- 3 cups all-purpose flour
- 1 teaspoon baking soda
- 3/4 cup thawed lemonade concentrate, *divided*

Additional sugar

- In a large bowl, cream butter and sugar until light and fluffy. Add eggs, one at a time, beating well after each addition. Combine flour and baking soda; add to the creamed mixture alternately with 1/3 cup lemonade concentrate, beating well after each addition.
- Drop by rounded teaspoonfuls onto ungreased baking sheets. Bake at 400° for 8 minutes. Remove to wire racks. Brush with remaining lemonade concentrate; sprinkle with sugar. Cool.

YIELD: 6 DOZEN.

tip
crispy or chewy?

If you prefer crisp oatmeal cookies, add 1/2 cup of broken sugar-frosted cornflakes to your dough for an unexpected crunch. If you go for moister, softer cookies, add a few chopped mashed ripe bananas to the dough.

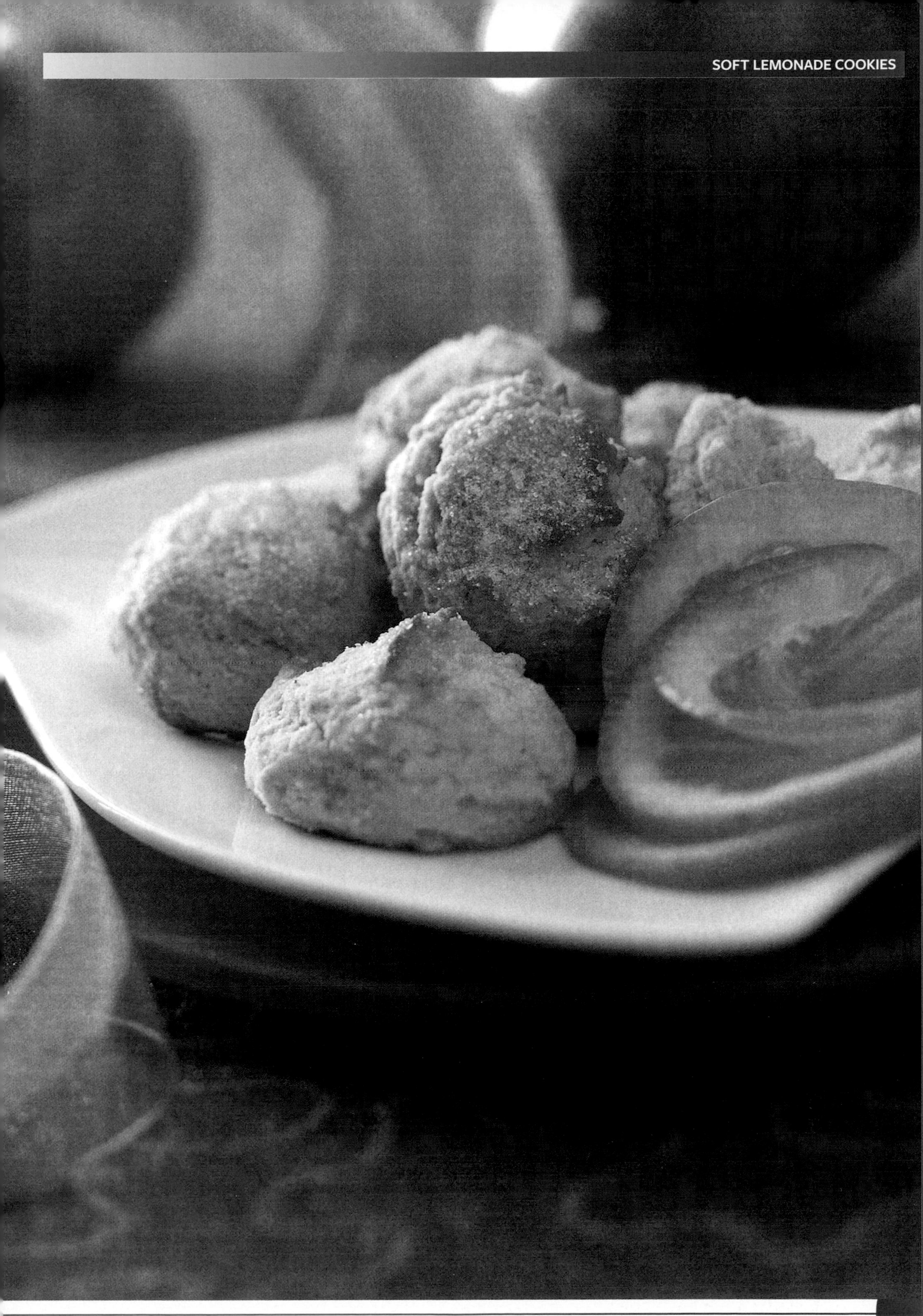

pumpkin chocolate chip cookies

PREP 10 min.
BAKE 15 min. + cooling

MARIETTA SLATER • JUSTIN, TEXAS

I'm one of the cooking project leaders for my daughter's 4-H club. These soft, delicious cookies are always a big hit with the kids.

1	cup butter, softened
3/4	cup sugar
3/4	cup packed brown sugar
1	egg
1	teaspoon vanilla extract
2	cups all-purpose flour
1	cup quick-cooking oats
1	teaspoon baking soda
1	teaspoon ground cinnamon
1	cup canned pumpkin
1-1/2	cups semisweet chocolate chips

• In a bowl, cream butter and sugars until light and fluffy. Beat in egg and vanilla. Combine the flour, oats, baking soda and cinnamon; stir into creamed mixture alternately with pumpkin. Fold in chocolate chips.

• Drop by tablespoonfuls onto greased baking sheets. Bake at 350° for 12-13 minutes or until lightly browned. Remove to wire racks to cool.

YIELD: 4 DOZEN.

CHOCOLATE-PEANUT BUTTER COOKIES

PUMPKIN CHOCOLATE CHIP COOKIES

chocolate-peanut butter cookies

PREP 15 min.
BAKE 10 min.

ELAINE STEPHENS • CARMEL, INDIANA

Kids will love making these easy bites with mom, dad or the grandparents. They're dense, rich and absolutely perfect for dunking in a cold glass of milk!

2	cans (16 ounces *each*) chocolate fudge frosting, *divided*
1	egg
1	cup chunky peanut butter
1-1/2	cups all-purpose flour
	Granulated sugar

• Set aside one can plus 1/3 cup frosting. In a large bowl, combine the egg, peanut butter and remaining frosting. Stir in flour just until moistened.

• Drop by rounded tablespoonfuls 2 in. apart on baking sheets coated with cooking spray. Flatten cookies with a fork dipped in sugar.

• Bake at 375° for 8-11 minutes or until set. Remove to wire racks. Cool completely; spread with reserved frosting.

YIELD: 3-1/2 DOZEN.

full-of-chips cookies

PREP 15 min.
BAKE 10 min. + cooling

DOLORES HARTFORD • TROY, PENNSYLVANIA

My mom created this special recipe for my daughter after she asked her if she could create a cookie filled with all of her favorite ingredients. These delightful gems were the tasty result.

1	cup butter-flavored shortening
3/4	cup sugar
3/4	cup packed brown sugar
2	eggs
1	teaspoon vanilla extract
2-1/4	cups all-purpose flour
1	teaspoon baking soda
3/4	teaspoon salt
1/3	cup *each* semisweet chocolate chips, peanut butter chips, butterscotch chips and white baking chips
1/3	cup milk chocolate M&M's
1/3	cup Reese's pieces candy

• In a large bowl, cream shortening and sugars until light and fluffy. Add eggs, one at a time, beating well after each addition. Beat in vanilla.

Combine the flour, baking soda and salt; gradually add to creamed mixture and mix well. Stir in chips and candy.

• Drop by rounded tablespoonfuls 2 in. apart onto ungreased baking sheets. Bake at 375° for 7-9 minutes or until lightly browned around edges. Remove to wire racks to cool.

YIELD: ABOUT 4 DOZEN.

chewy chocolate cookies

PREP 20 min.
BAKE 10 min.

LOUISE MILLER • BINSCARTH, MANITOBA

"No one can eat just one" definitely applies to this chewy, chocolaty cookie. It's an all-time favorite with family, friends and 4-H members.

- 1-1/4 cups butter, softened
- 2 cups sugar
- 2 eggs
- 2 teaspoons vanilla extract
- 2 cups sifted all-purpose flour
- 3/4 cup baking cocoa
- 1 teaspoon baking soda
- 1/2 teaspoon salt
- 1-1/2 cups semisweet chocolate chips
- 1/2 cup finely chopped walnuts *or* pecans

• In a large bowl, cream butter and sugar until light and fluffy. Beat in eggs and vanilla.

• Combine the flour, cocoa, baking soda and salt; gradually add to creamed mixture and mix well. Stir in chocolate chips and nuts. Drop by teaspoonfuls onto ungreased baking sheets.

• Bake at 350° for 8-9 minutes or until edges are set. Cool on pans for 1 minute before removing to wire racks.

YIELD: 4 DOZEN.

potato chip cookies

PREP 15 min.
BAKE 10 min.

MONNA LU BAUER • LEXINGTON, KENTUCKY

Give these cookies a try the next time you're looking for a sweet and salty treat! They quickly bake to a crispy, golden brown...and they will disappear even faster!

- 1 cup butter-flavored shortening
- 3/4 cup sugar
- 3/4 cup packed brown sugar
- 2 eggs
- 2 cups all-purpose flour
- 1 teaspoon baking soda
- 2 cups crushed potato chips
- 1 cup butterscotch chips

• In a large bowl, cream shortening and sugars until light and fluffy. Beat in eggs. Combine flour and baking soda; gradually add to creamed mixture and mix well. Stir in potato chips and butterscotch chips.

• Drop by tablespoonfuls 2 in. apart onto ungreased baking sheets. Bake at 375° for 10-12 minutes or until golden brown. Cool for 1 minute before removing to wire racks.

YIELD: 4 DOZEN.

carrot cookie bites

PREP 15 min.
BAKE 10 min.

JEANIE PETRIK • GREENSBURG, KENTUCKY

This recipe is a longtime family favorite. The cookies are soft and delicious, and the aroma while baking is absolutely irresistible! I'm always asked for the recipe.

- 2/3 cup shortening
- 1 cup packed brown sugar
- 2 eggs
- 1/2 cup buttermilk
- 1 teaspoon vanilla extract
- 2 cups all-purpose flour
- 1 teaspoon ground cinnamon
- 1/2 teaspoon salt
- 1/4 teaspoon baking powder
- 1/4 teaspoon baking soda
- 1/4 teaspoon ground nutmeg
- 1/4 teaspoon ground cloves
- 2 cups quick-cooking oats
- 1 cup shredded carrots
- 1/2 cup chopped pecans

• In a large bowl, cream shortening and brown sugar until light and fluffy. Beat in the eggs, buttermilk and vanilla. Combine the flour, cinnamon, salt, baking powder, baking soda, nutmeg and cloves; gradually add to creamed mixture. Stir in the oats, carrots, and pecans.

• To freeze the cookie dough, drop desired amount of dough by rounded teaspoonfuls onto baking sheets; cover and freeze until firm. Transfer frozen cookie dough balls into a resealable plastic freezer bag. May be frozen for up to 3 months.

• Drop remaining cookie dough by rounded teaspoonfuls 2 in. apart onto ungreased baking sheets. Bake at 375° for 6-8 minutes or until lightly browned. Remove to wire racks to cool.

• **TO USE FROZEN COOKIE DOUGH:** Place the dough balls 2 in. apart onto ungreased baking sheets. Bake at 375° for 10-15 minutes or until lightly browned. Remove to wire racks to cool.

YIELD: 7 DOZEN.

CARROT COOKIE BITES

COCONUT CRUNCH COOKIES

gradually add to butter mixture and mix well. Stir in cranberries and chips.

- Drop by heaping tablespoonfuls 2 in. apart onto baking sheets coated with cooking spray. Bake at 375° for 8-10 minutes or until lightly browned. Cool for 1 minute before removing to wire racks.

YIELD: 2 DOZEN.

cocoa marshmallow cookies

PREP 25 min.
BAKE 10 min.

LYNELL RENNER • ZAP, NORTH DAKOTA

It was always a treat when Mom made these goodies when I was growing up. I usually double the recipe because they disappear so fast. The marshmallow is a nice surprise under the sweet frosting.

- 1 cup sugar
- 1/2 cup shortening
- 1 egg
- 1/4 cup 2% milk
- 1-3/4 cups all-purpose flour
- 1/2 cup baking cocoa
- 1 teaspoon baking soda
- 1/2 teaspoon salt
- 12 large marshmallows, halved

FROSTING:
- 2 cups confectioners' sugar
- 2 tablespoons baking cocoa
- 1 tablespoon butter, softened
- 3 to 4 tablespoons 2% milk

- In a large bowl, cream sugar and shortening until light and fluffy. Beat in egg and milk. Combine the flour, cocoa, baking soda and salt; add to creamed mixture and mix well.

- Drop by teaspoonfuls onto ungreased baking sheets. Bake at 350° for 8 minutes. Place half of a marshmallow on each cookie; bake 2 minutes longer.

- Remove cookies from the oven and press the marshmallows down with a fork. Cool. Meanwhile, for frosting, in a large bowl, combine the confectioners' sugar, cocoa, butter and enough milk to reach desired spreading consistency. Frost the cookies.

YIELD: 2 DOZEN.

coconut crunch cookies

PREP 30 min.
BAKE 10 min.

MARIA REGAKIS • SOMERVILLE, MASSACHUSETTS

These sweet drop cookies are loaded with coconut and chocolate chips. Their crisp edges and soft centers add up to a perfect cookie.

- 1 cup butter, softened
- 3/4 cup sugar
- 3/4 cup packed brown sugar
- 2 eggs
- 2 teaspoons vanilla extract
- 1 teaspoon almond extract
- 2 cups all-purpose flour
- 1 teaspoon baking soda
- 3/4 teaspoon salt
- 2 cups flaked coconut
- 1 package (11-1/2 ounces) milk chocolate chips
- 1-1/2 cups finely chopped almonds

- In a large bowl, cream butter and sugars until light and fluffy. Beat in eggs and extracts. Combine the flour, baking soda and salt; gradually add to creamed mixture and mix well. Stir in the coconut, chocolate chips and almonds.

- Drop by rounded teaspoonfuls 2 in. apart onto ungreased baking sheets. Bake at 375°

for 9-11 minutes or until lightly browned. Cool for 1 minute before removing from pans to wire racks.

YIELD: ABOUT 4-1/2 DOZEN.

white chocolate cranberry cookies

PREP 20 min.
BAKE 10 min.

DONNA BECK • SCOTTDALE, PENNSYLVANIA

These sweet gems feature white chocolate and cranberries for a delightful taste. The red and white colors add a festive feel to any dessert tray.

- 1/3 cup butter, softened
- 1/2 cup packed brown sugar
- 1/3 cup sugar
- 1 egg
- 1 teaspoon vanilla extract
- 1-1/2 cups all-purpose flour
- 1/2 teaspoon salt
- 1/2 teaspoon baking soda
- 3/4 cup dried cranberries
- 1/2 cup white baking chips

- In a large bowl, beat butter and sugars until crumbly, about 2 minutes. Beat in egg and vanilla. Combine the flour, salt and baking soda;

frosted gingerbread nut cookies

PREP 15 min.
BAKE 10 min. + cooling

KARYN ROGERS • HEMET, CALIFORNIA

I received the recipe for these soft ginger cookies from a dear friend, who has since passed away. A comforting classic like this always satisfies my sweet tooth.

- 1/2 cup butter, softened
- 2/3 cup sugar
- 1 egg
- 1/2 cup molasses
- 2-3/4 cups all-purpose flour
- 1 teaspoon baking soda
- 1 teaspoon ground cinnamon
- 1 teaspoon ground ginger
- 1/2 teaspoon salt
- 1/4 teaspoon ground cloves
- 1/2 cup buttermilk
- 1/2 cup chopped walnuts

FROSTING:

- 1-1/2 cups confectioners' sugar
- 4-1/2 teaspoons butter, softened
- 1/2 teaspoon vanilla extract
- 2 to 3 tablespoons half-and-half cream

Walnuts halves, optional

- In a large bowl, cream butter and sugar until light and fluffy. Beat in egg and molasses. Combine the flour, baking soda, cinnamon, ginger, salt and cloves; add to creamed mixture alternately with buttermilk, beating well after each addition. Stir in chopped walnuts.

- Drop by tablespoonfuls 2 in. apart onto greased baking sheets. Bake at 350° for 10-12 minutes or until edges are firm. Remove to wire racks to cool.

- For the frosting, in a small bowl, combine the confectioners' sugar, butter, vanilla and enough cream to achieve desired consistency. Frost cooled cookies. Top each with a walnut half if desired.

YIELD: 5 DOZEN.

chocolate pecan kisses

PREP 15 min. + standing
BAKE 40 min. + standing

JOSEPHINE BEALS • ZIONSVILLE, INDIANA

A good friend gave me this recipe and I, in turn, have shared it with many others. It's a very easy recipe and it makes a lot of cookies. They are sometimes called "forgotten" cookies because you can bake them at night and leave them in the oven until the next morning.

- 1 egg white
- 1/3 cup sugar

CHOCOLATE PECAN KISSES

- 1/2 cup miniature semisweet chocolate chips
- 1/2 cup chopped pecans

- Place egg white in a small bowl; let stand at room temperature for 30 minutes. Beat on medium speed until soft peaks form. Gradually beat in sugar, 1 tablespoon at a time, on high until stiff peaks form. Fold in chocolate chips and pecans.

- Drop by rounded teaspoonfuls 2 in. apart onto parchment paper-lined baking sheets. Bake at 250° for 40-45 minutes or until firm to the touch. Turn oven off and let cookies dry in the oven for 1-1/2 hours.

- Carefully remove cookies from parchment paper. Store in an airtight container.

YIELD: 1-1/2 DOZEN.

FROSTED GINGERBREAD NUT COOKIES

tip

meringue cookies

Here are some quick and easy tips for successful meringue cookies. For the greatest volume, place the egg white in a small clean metal or glass mixing bowl. Even a drop of fat from the egg yolk or a film sometimes found on plastic bowls will prevent egg whites from foaming. For this reason, be sure to use clean beaters. After stiff peaks form, check that the sugar is dissolved. It should feel silky smooth when rubbed between your thumb and index finger.

OATMEAL RAISIN COOKIES

oatmeal raisin cookies

PREP 15 min.
BAKE 15 min.

SANDI SWARTZENBERGER • KALISPELL, MONTANA

In my small neighborhood, my grandkids and their friends stop by throughout the day. I keep my cookie jar well supplied with these classic treats.

- 2 cups butter, softened
- 2 cups packed brown sugar
- 1 cup sugar
- 2 eggs
- 1/2 cup water
- 2 teaspoons vanilla extract
- 6 cups quick-cooking oats
- 2-1/2 cups all-purpose flour
- 2 teaspoons salt
- 2 teaspoons ground cinnamon
- 1 teaspoon baking soda
- 2-1/2 cups raisins
- 2 cups (12 ounces) semisweet chocolate chips
- 1-1/2 cups chopped walnuts
- 1 cup flaked coconut

● In a large bowl, cream butter and sugars until light and fluffy. Add eggs, one at a time, beating well after each addition. Beat in water and vanilla. Combine the oats, flour, salt, cinnamon and baking soda; gradually add to creamed mixture and mix well. (Transfer to a larger bowl if necessary.) Stir in the raisins, chocolate chips, walnuts and coconut.

● Drop by tablespoonfuls 2 in. apart onto ungreased baking sheets. Bake at 350° for 12-14 minutes or until lightly browned. Remove to wire racks to cool.

YIELD: ABOUT 12-1/2 DOZEN.

jumbo chocolate chip cookies

PREP 15 min. + chilling
BAKE 15 min.

LORI SPORER • OAKLEY, KANSAS

These huge cookies are a family favorite. No one can resist their sweet chocolaty taste.

- 2/3 cup shortening
- 2/3 cup butter, softened
- 1 cup sugar
- 1 cup packed brown sugar
- 2 eggs
- 2 teaspoons vanilla extract
- 3-1/2 cups all-purpose flour
- 1 teaspoon baking soda
- 1 teaspoon salt
- 2 cups (12 ounces) semisweet chocolate chips
- 1 cup chopped pecans

● In a large bowl, cream shortening, butter and sugars until light and fluffy. Beat in eggs and vanilla. Combine the flour, baking soda and salt; add to creamed mixture and mix well. Fold in the chocolate chips and pecans. Chill for at least 1 hour.

● Drop by 1/4 cupfuls at least 1-1/2 in. apart onto greased baking sheets. Bake at 375° for 13-15 minutes or until golden brown. Cool for 5 minutes before removing to a wire rack.

YIELD: 2 DOZEN.

JUMBO CHOCOLATE CHIP COOKIES

chocolate lover's dream cookies

PREP 15 min.

BAKE 15 min.

PAULA ZSIRAY • LOGAN, UTAH

These rich chocolate cookies with white chips are so scrumptious. My young daughter won 1st prize in the cookie division of a local Chocolate Festival with this recipe.

- 6 tablespoons canola oil
- 1/4 cup butter, softened
- 3/4 cup packed brown sugar
- 1/2 cup sugar
- 2 eggs
- 1 teaspoon vanilla extract
- 1-1/4 cups all-purpose flour
- 1/2 cup baking cocoa
- 1/4 teaspoon baking powder
- 1 cup white baking chips
- 1 cup (6 ounces) semisweet chocolate chips

• In a large bowl, beat the oil, butter and sugars until well blended. Add eggs, one at a time, beating well after each addition. Beat in vanilla. Combine the flour, cocoa and baking powder; gradually add to oil mixture and mix well. Stir in chips.

• Drop by rounded tablespoonfuls 2 in. apart onto ungreased baking sheets. Bake at 350° for 12-15 minutes or until edges begin to brown. Cool for 1 minute before removing from pans to wire racks.

YIELD: 3-1/2 DOZEN.

toffee meringue drops

PREP 25 min.

BAKE 25 min. + standing

BETTE RICHARDS • CALEDONIA, ONTARIO

The original recipe called for mini chocolate chips and crushed peppermint candy. I didn't have those ingredients on hand so I substituted toffee bits. Everyone loved the tasty results!

- 2 egg whites
- 1/8 teaspoon cream of tartar
- 1/2 cup sugar
- 1/2 cup milk chocolate English toffee bits
- 1/2 cup finely chopped pecans

CHOCOLATE LOVER'S DREAM COOKIES

• In a large bowl, beat egg whites and cream of tartar on medium speed until soft peaks form. Gradually add sugar, 1 tablespoon at a time, beating on high until stiff glossy peaks form and sugar is dissolved, about 6 minutes. Fold in toffee bits and pecans.

• Drop by tablespoonfuls 2 in. apart onto parchment paper-lined baking sheets. Bake at 250° for 25-30 minutes or until set and dry. Turn oven off; leave cookies in oven for 1 hour.

• Cool completely on pans on wire racks.

YIELD: 3 DOZEN.

pineapple delights

PREP 15 min.

BAKE 10 min.

JACK STUBBLEFIELD • EAST CANTON, OHIO

My mother would often send these treats to me when I was stationed in Germany. The recipe was my grandmother's, and now my wife and daughter bake them, too.

- 1 cup butter, softened
- 1 cup sugar
- 1 cup packed brown sugar
- 2 eggs
- 1 teaspoon vanilla extract
- 4 cups all-purpose flour
- 2 teaspoons baking powder
- 1/2 teaspoon baking soda
- 1/2 teaspoon salt
- 1 can (8 ounces) unsweetened crushed pineapple, drained
- 1 cup chopped walnuts
- 1/4 cup chopped maraschino cherries

• In a large bowl, cream butter and sugars until light and fluffy. Add the eggs, one at a time, beating well after each addition. Beat in vanilla. Combine the flour, baking powder, baking soda and salt; gradually add to the creamed mixture and mix well. Stir in the pineapple, walnuts and cherries.

• Drop by rounded tablespoonfuls 2 in. apart onto ungreased baking sheets. Bake at 425° for 7-9 minutes or until lightly browned. Remove to wire racks to cool.

YIELD: 7 DOZEN.

slice & bake cookies

If you have a passion for baking but are short on time, you'll love the assortment of traditional refrigerator cookies offered here.

RAINBOW BUTTER COOKIES

rainbow butter cookies

PREP 30 min. + chilling
BAKE 10 min.

LANETTE TATE • SANDY, UTAH

These colorful cookies make great classroom or birthday snacks as kids are enchanted by the rainbow of colors.

- 1/2 cup plus 2 tablespoons butter, softened
- 1/2 cup packed brown sugar
- 1/4 cup sugar
- 1 egg
- 1 teaspoon vanilla extract
- 2 cups all-purpose flour
- 1/2 teaspoon baking powder
- 1/2 teaspoon salt
- 1/8 teaspoon baking soda
- Green, red and yellow food coloring
- Milk

• In a large bowl, cream butter and sugars until light and fluffy. Add egg and vanilla. Combine the flour, baking powder, salt and baking soda; gradually add to creamed mixture and mix well.

• Divide dough into three portions; tint each a different color. Roll each portion of dough on waxed paper into a 9-in. x 5-in. rectangle. Freeze for 10 minutes.

• Cut each rectangle in half lengthwise. Lightly brush top of one rectangle with milk. Top with another colored dough. Remove waxed paper; brush top with milk. Repeat with remaining dough, alternating colors to make six layers. Press together lightly; cut in half lengthwise. Wrap each with plastic wrap. Refrigerate for several hours or overnight.

• Unwrap dough; cut into 1/8-in. slices. Place 2 in. apart on ungreased baking sheets. Bake at 350° for 8-10 minutes. Cool for 1-2 minutes before removing from pans to wire racks to cool completely.

YIELD: ABOUT 4 DOZEN.

lemon angel wings

PREP 20 min. + chilling
BAKE 20 min. + cooling

CHAROLETTE WESTFALL • HOUSTON, TEXAS

You are sure to fall in love with the light, lemony flavor of these angel wings. They make an impressive treat served alongside tea.

- 1-1/2 cups all-purpose flour
- 1 cup cold butter, cubed
- 1/2 cup sour cream
- 1 teaspoon grated lemon peel
- 10 tablespoons sugar, *divided*

• Place flour in a large bowl; cut in butter until crumbly. Stir in sour cream and lemon peel until well blended. Place on a piece of waxed paper; shape into a 4-1/2-in. square. Wrap in plastic wrap and refrigerate for at least 2 hours.

• Cut the dough into four 2-1/4-in. squares. Place one square on a piece of waxed paper sprinkled with 2 tablespoons of sugar. Cover with another piece of waxed paper. Keep remaining squares refrigerated. Roll out dough into a 12-in. x 5-in. rectangle, turning often to coat both sides with sugar.

• Lightly mark the center of 12-in. side. Starting with a short side, roll up jelly-roll style to the center mark, peeling waxed paper away while rolling. Repeat rolling from other short side, so the two rolls meet in the center and resemble a scroll.

• Wrap in plastic wrap and refrigerate. Repeat with remaining squares, using 2 tablespoons sugar for each. Chill for 1 hour.

• Unwrap dough and cut into 1/2-in. slices; dip each side in remaining sugar. Place 2 in. apart on foil-lined baking sheets. Bake at 375° for 14 minutes or until golden brown. Turn cookies over; bake 5 minutes longer. Remove to wire racks to cool.

YIELD: 3 DOZEN.

LEMON ANGEL WINGS

lemon thins

PREP 35 min. + chilling
BAKE 10 min. + cooling

JUDY WILSON • SUN CITY WEST, ARIZONA

These irresistible thins have a tart lemon taste and a crisp texture. To create a simple but special dessert, place some of the cookies in bowls of chocolate or vanilla ice cream.

- 1/3 cup butter, softened
- 1/3 cup shortening
- 1 cup sugar
- 2 tablespoons lemon juice
- 2 teaspoons grated lemon peel
- 1/2 teaspoon lemon extract
- 1/2 teaspoon vanilla extract
- 1-1/2 cups all-purpose flour
- 1-1/2 teaspoons baking powder
- 1/2 teaspoon baking soda
- 1/4 teaspoon salt
- 2 tablespoons confectioners' sugar

• In a large bowl, cream the butter, shortening and sugar until light and fluffy. Beat in the lemon juice, lemon peel and extracts.

• Combine the flour, baking powder, baking soda and salt; gradually add to the creamed mixture and mix well. Shape into a 12-in. roll; wrap in plastic wrap. Refrigerate for at least 2 hours or until firm.

• Unwrap dough; cut into 1/4-in. slices. Place 2 in. apart on ungreased baking sheets.

• Bake at 350° for 8-9 minutes or until edges are lightly browned. Cool for 1-2 minutes before removing from pans to wire racks to cool completely. Dust with confectioners' sugar.

YIELD: 4-1/2 DOZEN.

SLICE & BAKE ORANGE SPICE WAFERS

slice & bake orange spice wafers

PREP 45 min. + chilling
BAKE 5 min.

TASTE OF HOME TEST KITCHEN

These slim and crunchy wafers stack well, making them a great gift to send to a loved one. Ginger and orange combine for a sweet and spicy flavor.

- 1 cup butter, softened
- 3/4 cup sugar
- 3/4 cup packed brown sugar
- 1 egg
- 2 tablespoons light corn syrup
- 3 cups all-purpose flour
- 2 teaspoons baking soda
- 2 teaspoons ground ginger
- 2 teaspoons grated orange peel
- 1/4 teaspoon *each* ground allspice, cloves and nutmeg

Additional sugar, optional

• In a large bowl, cream butter and sugars until light and fluffy. Beat in egg and corn syrup. Combine the flour, baking soda, ginger, orange peel, allspice, cloves and nutmeg; gradually add to creamed mixture and mix well.

• Shape into four 6-in. rolls; wrap in plastic wrap. Refrigerate overnight.

• Unwrap and cut into 1/8-in. slices. Place 2 in. apart on ungreased baking sheets. Sprinkle with additional sugar if desired.

• Bake at 400° for 5-6 minutes or until lightly browned. Remove to wire racks to cool.

YIELD: 16 DOZEN.

cherry icebox cookies

PREP 20 min. + chilling
BAKE 10 min.

PATTY COURTNEY • JONESBORO, TEXAS

Maraschino cherries add colorful flecks to icebox cookies. These cute little bites make great treats for Christmas or Valentine's Day.

- 1 cup butter, softened
- 1 cup sugar
- 1/4 cup packed brown sugar
- 1 egg
- 1/4 cup maraschino cherry juice
- 4-1/2 teaspoons lemon juice
- 1 teaspoon vanilla extract
- 3-1/4 cups all-purpose flour
- 1/2 teaspoon baking soda
- 1/2 teaspoon ground cinnamon
- 1/4 teaspoon cream of tartar
- 1/2 cup chopped walnuts
- 1/2 cup chopped maraschino cherries

• In a large bowl, cream butter and sugars until light and fluffy. Beat in the egg, cherry and lemon juices and vanilla. Combine the dry ingredients; gradually add to creamed mixture and mix well. Stir in nuts and cherries.

• Shape into four 12-in. rolls; wrap each in plastic wrap. Refrigerate for 4 hours or until firm.

• Unwrap and cut into 1/4-in. slices. Place 2 in. apart on ungreased baking sheets. Bake at 375° for 8-10 minutes or until the edges begin to brown. Remove to wire racks to cool.

YIELD: ABOUT 6 DOZEN.

LEMON THINS

LEMON POPPY SEED SLICES

lemon poppy seed slices

PREP 10 min. + chilling
BAKE 10 min.

PAULINE PIRAINO • BAY SHORE, NEW YORK

My mom taught me to bake, and I use lots of recipes from her abundant collection, including this one.

  3/4 cup butter, softened
    1 cup sugar
    1 egg
    1 tablespoon 2% milk
    2 teaspoons finely grated lemon peel
  1/2 teaspoon vanilla extract
  1/2 teaspoon lemon extract, optional
2-1/2 cups all-purpose flour
  1/4 cup poppy seeds

• In a large bowl, cream butter and sugar until light and fluffy. Beat in egg, milk, lemon peel and extracts. Gradually add flour and mix well. Stir in poppy seeds.

• Shape into two 8-in. rolls; wrap each in plastic wrap. Refrigerate for 3 hours or until firm. Unwrap and cut into 1/4-in. slice. Place 2 in. apart on ungreased baking sheets.

tip

lemon peel

A quick and easy way to make finely grated lemon peel for recipes is to slice off big pieces of peel and grind them for just a few seconds in a food processor.

• Bake at 350° for 10-12 minutes or until edges are golden. Cool for 2 minutes before removing to wire racks to cool completely.

YIELD: 5-1/2 DOZEN.

chocolate mint surprises

PREP 30 min. + chilling
BAKE 5 min. + freezing

SHEILA KERR • REVELSTOKE, BRITISH COLUMBIA

I came up with this recipe a few years ago and have shared it with many people. I would often snack on these goodies after my baby's middle-of-the-night feeding.

  3/4 cup butter, softened
    1 cup sugar
    1 egg
    1 teaspoon vanilla extract
    3 ounces unsweetened chocolate, melted and cooled
2-1/2 cups all-purpose flour
1-1/2 teaspoons baking powder
  1/2 teaspoon salt

MINT FILLING:

    4 cups confectioners' sugar
    3 tablespoons butter, softened
  1/4 cup evaporated milk
    2 to 3 teaspoons peppermint extract
  1/2 teaspoon vanilla extract
    2 pounds dark chocolate candy coating, melted

• In a large bowl, cream butter and sugar until light and fluffy. Beat in egg and vanilla. Add melted chocolate. Combine the flour, baking powder and salt; gradually add to chocolate mixture and mix well. Shape in two 10-in. rolls; wrap each in plastic wrap. Refrigerate for 4 hours or until firm.

• Unwrap the dough and cut into 1/4-in. slices. Place 2 in. apart on ungreased baking sheets. Bake at 375° for 5-7 minutes or until edges are firm. Remove to wire racks to cool.

• For the filling, in a small bowl, combine the confectioners' sugar, butter, milk and extracts until smooth. Shape into 1/2-in. balls. Place a ball in the center of each cookie; flatten. Freeze for 30 minutes.

• Dip the cookies in the melted candy coating to completely cover; allow excess to drip off. Place on waxed paper; let stand until set.

YIELD: ABOUT 6 DOZEN.

CHOCOLATE MINT SURPRISES

date nut icebox cookies

PREP 15 min. + chilling
BAKE 10 min.

GLADYS MAURER • LARAMIE, WYOMING

A dear friend shared this recipe with me many years ago. These cookies quickly became a much-requested treat at my house, so it's a good thing the recipe yields a large batch!

- 1 cup butter, softened
- 1 cup shortening
- 2-1/2 cups sugar
- 2 eggs
- 1-1/2 teaspoons vanilla extract
- 1 tablespoon light corn syrup
- 5 cups all-purpose flour
- 1 teaspoon salt
- 1 teaspoon baking soda
- 1 cup finely chopped walnuts
- 1 cup finely chopped dates

- In a large bowl, cream butter, shortening and sugar until light and fluffy. Add eggs, one at a time, beating well after each addition. Beat in vanilla and corn syrup. Combine the flour, salt and baking soda; gradually add to the creamed mixture and mix well. Stir in walnuts and dates.

- Shape into four 6-in. rolls; wrap each in plastic wrap. Refrigerate overnight.

- Unwrap and cut into 1/4-in. slices. Place 2-1/2 in. apart on ungreased baking sheets. Bake at 375° for 10-12 minutes or until lightly browned. Cool for 2-3 minutes before removing to wire racks.

YIELD: ABOUT 8 DOZEN.

pastelitos de boda

PREP 20 min. + chilling
BAKE 15 min.

TERRI LINS • SAN DIEGO, CALIFORNIA

In Mexico, these rich cookies are called Little Wedding Cakes. I enjoy trying authentic recipes—they're a sharp departure from the Iowa favorites I grew up with!

- 3/4 cup butter, softened
- 1/2 cup confectioners' sugar
- 2 teaspoons vanilla
- 2 cups sifted all-purpose flour
- 1/4 teaspoon salt

DATE NUT ICEBOX COOKIES

- 1 cup finely chopped walnuts
- 1/4 cup heavy whipping cream
- Additional confectioners' sugar

- In a large bowl, cream the butter and sugar; add vanilla. Combine the flour, salt and nuts; gradually add to creamed mixture. Add cream; knead lightly.

- Shape into a roll 2-1/2 in. in diameter. Wrap in plastic wrap. Refrigerate for several hours or overnight.

- Unwrap and cut into 1/4-in. slices. Place 2 in. apart on ungreased baking sheets. Bake at 375° for 15 minutes or until delicately browned around edges. Remove to wire racks. While warm, roll in additional confectioners' sugar.

YIELD: ABOUT 3 DOZEN.

slice-and-bake cookies

PREP 15 min. + chilling
BAKE 10 min.

MONICA GIBBONS • DAYTON, OHIO

I love this cookie dough because it's so versatile. Add any kind of chips or nuts to suit your tastes.

- 1 cup shortening
- 3/4 cup packed brown sugar
- 3/4 cup sugar
- 2 eggs
- 1 teaspoon vanilla extract
- 2-1/4 cups all-purpose flour
- 1 teaspoon salt
- 1 teaspoon baking soda
- 1-1/2 cups "extras" (any one *or* combination of the following: chocolate, butterscotch, toffee *or* peanut butter chips, chopped candied cherries *or* nuts)

- In a bowl, cream shortening and sugars. Add eggs and vanilla. Combine flour, salt and baking soda; add to the creamed mixture and mix well. Fold in 1-1/2 cups "extras." Shape into a 15-in. x 2-in. roll; wrap tightly with plastic wrap. Chill 2 hours or up to 1 week.

- To bake, cut dough into 1/2-in. slices. Place 3 in. apart onto ungreased baking sheets. Bake at 350° for 10 minutes. Cool for 5 minutes; remove to wire racks.

YIELD: 2-1/2 DOZEN.

versatile slice 'n' bake cookies

PREP 20 min.
BAKE 15 min. + cooling

TASTE OF HOME TEST KITCHEN

When you crave a sweet treat or want something fun and festive to make with the little ones, pull this frozen cookie dough from the freezer, slice and pop in the oven. Once baked, these buttery, melt-in-your-mouth delights from our Test Kitchen staff will keep for a week...but they'll probably disappear much faster!

- 1 cup butter, softened
- 1 cup sugar
- 1/4 teaspoon vanilla extract
- 1-3/4 cups all-purpose flour
- 3/4 teaspoon baking soda
- 1/4 teaspoon salt
- 2 tablespoons chopped mixed candied fruit, optional

Nonpareils, jimmies, melted semisweet chocolate chips and chopped nuts, optional

- In a small bowl, cream butter and sugar until light and fluffy. Beat in vanilla. Combine the flour, baking soda and salt; gradually add to creamed mixture and mix well.

- Divide into three portions. If desired, add candied fruit to one portion. Shape each into a 5-in. roll; place in a freezer bag. Seal and freeze for up to 3 months.

- **TO USE FROZEN DOUGH:** Remove from the freezer 1 hour before baking. Unwrap and cut into 1/4-in. slices. Place 2 in. apart on baking sheets coated with cooking spray. Sprinkle with nonpareils and jimmies if desired.

- Bake at 350° for 12-14 minutes or until set. Remove to wire racks to cool. Frost with melted chocolate chips and sprinkle with nuts if desired.

YIELD: 4-1/2 DOZEN.

shortbread

PREP 15 min. + chilling
BAKE 15 min.

MRS. ALLEN SWENSON • CAMDETON, MISSOURI

I live in Missouri, but many of my "family tradition" recipes come from New Zealand. My parents moved there when I was 1, and that's where I grew up, so many in my collection have a "Down Under" heritage. These special-occasion cookies bring back warm memories of my childhood, and I'm going to make sure they're passed on to the next generation in my family...no matter where they live!

- 1 cup butter, softened
- 1/2 cup sugar
- 1/2 cup confectioners' sugar
- 1/2 teaspoon salt
- 2 cups all-purpose flour
- 1/2 cup cornstarch

- In bowl, cream the butter, sugars and salt until light and fluffy. Combine the flour and cornstarch; gradually add to creamed mixture. Roll dough into a 15-in. x 2-in. x 1-in. rectangle; chill in the refrigerator.

- Cut into 1/4-in. slices; place on ungreased baking sheets. Prick with a fork. Bake at 325° for 15-18 minutes. Don't overbake—cookies will not brown. Remove to wire racks to cool.

YIELD: 5 DOZEN.

pecan icebox cookies

PREP 15 min. + chilling
BAKE 10 min.

ANGI ROGMAN • SEATTLE, WASHINGTON

My best friend's grandmother frequently makes these old-fashioned icebox gems and was kind enough to pass the treasured family recipe on to me.

- 1 cup butter, softened
- 1 cup sugar
- 1 cup packed brown sugar
- 3 eggs
- 4 cups all-purpose flour
- 2 teaspoons baking powder
- 1 teaspoon baking soda
- 1 teaspoon ground cinnamon
- 1/2 teaspoon salt
- 1 cup chopped pecans

- In a large bowl, cream butter and sugars until light and fluffy. Add the eggs, one at time, beating well after each addition. Combine the flour, baking powder, baking soda, cinnamon and salt; gradually add to the creamed mixture and mix well. Stir in pecans. Shape into four 6-1/2-in. rolls; wrap each in plastic wrap. Refrigerate overnight.

- Unwrap and cut into 1/8-in. slices. Place 1 in. apart on ungreased baking sheets. Bake at 375° for 7-10 minutes or until lightly browned. Remove to wire racks to cool.

YIELD: ABOUT 9 DOZEN.

VERSATILE SLICE 'N' BAKE COOKIES

WATERMELON COOKIES

caramel swirls

PREP 25 min. + chilling
BAKE 15 min.

JAN SMITH • STAR, TEXAS

In my opinion, nothing beats a plate full of cookies to satisfy your sweet tooth. With a nice, crisp outside and chewy caramel filling, these swirls are one of my favorites.

- 1 cup butter, softened
- 4 ounces cream cheese, softened
- 1 cup packed brown sugar
- 1 egg yolk
- 1 teaspoon maple flavoring
- 2-3/4 cups all-purpose flour

FILLING:

- 30 caramels
- 2 packages (3 ounces *each*) cream cheese, softened

• In a large bowl, cream the butter, cream cheese and brown sugar until light and fluffy. Beat in egg yolk and maple flavoring. Gradually add flour and mix well. Refrigerate for 2 hours or until easy to handle.

• In a microwave-safe bowl, melt caramels; stir until smooth. Stir in cream cheese until blended; set aside. Divide dough in half. Roll each portion between waxed paper to 1/4-in. thickness. Spread caramel mixture over dough to within 1/2 in. of edges.

• Tightly roll up jelly-roll style, starting with a long side. Wrap rolls in plastic wrap; refrigerate for 4 hours or until firm.

• Unwrap and cut into 1/4-in. slices. Place 1 in. apart on greased baking sheets. Bake at 350° for 12-14 minutes or until golden brown. Remove to wire racks to cool.

YIELD: 6-1/2 DOZEN.

CARAMEL SWIRLS

watermelon cookies

PREP 30 min. + chilling
BAKE 10 min. + cooling

RUTH WITMER • STEVENS, PENNSYLVANIA

I made these treats for a summer picnic, and they were gobbled up in a hurry! They may look like watermelons, but they actually feature the sweet taste of almond.

- 3/4 cup butter, cubed
- 3/4 cup sugar
- 1 egg
- 1/2 teaspoon almond extract
- 2-1/4 cups all-purpose flour
- 1/4 teaspoon salt
- 1/4 teaspoon baking powder
- Red and green food coloring
- Dried currants
- Sesame seeds

• In a large bowl, cream butter and sugar until light and fluffy. Beat in egg. Beat in extract. Combine the flour, salt and baking powder; gradually add to creamed mixture and mix well; set aside.

• Add enough of the red food coloring to tint remaining dough deep red. Roll into a 3-1/2-in.-long log; wrap in plastic wrap and refrigerate until firm, about 2 hours.

• Divide 1 cup of reserved dough into two pieces. To one piece, add enough green food coloring to tint dough deep green. Leave the remaining dough plain. Wrap each piece separately in plastic wrap; chill until firm, about 1 hour.

• On a floured sheet of waxed paper, roll white dough into an 8-1/2-in. x 3-1/2-in. rectangle. Place red dough along short end of rectangle. Roll up and encircle red dough with white dough; set aside.

• On floured waxed paper, roll the green dough into a 10-in. x 3-1/2-in. rectangle. Place log of red/white dough along the short end of green dough. Roll up and encircle log with green dough. Cover tightly with plastic wrap; refrigerate at least 8 hours or overnight.

• Unwrap the dough and cut into 1/8-in. slices. Place 1 in. apart on ungreased baking sheets. Lightly press the dried currants and sesame seeds into each slice to resemble watermelon seeds.

• Bake at 375° for 6-8 minutes or until cookies are firm but not brown. While still warm, cut each cookie in half or into pie-shaped wedges. Remove to wire racks to cool.

YIELD: 3 DOZEN.

aunt ione's icebox cookies

PREP 20 min. + chilling
BAKE 10 min.

JENNY HILL • MERIDIANVILLE, ALABAMA

Whenever we went to visit my Aunt Ione in Georgia, she would treat us to her famous icebox cookies.

- 6 cups all-purpose flour
- 1-1/2 teaspoons baking powder
- 1 teaspoon baking soda
- 1 teaspoon ground nutmeg
- 1 teaspoon ground cinnamon
- 2 cups butter, softened
- 1 cup sugar
- 1 cup packed brown sugar
- 3 eggs
- 1 teaspoon vanilla extract
- 1 teaspoon lemon extract
- 2 cups chopped nuts

- Sift together first five ingredients; set aside. In a bowl, cream butter and sugars. Add eggs, vanilla and lemon extract; beat well. Add dry ingredients; mix well. Stir in nuts.

- Divide dough into four parts and shape into 1-1/2-in. x 11-in. rolls. Wrap in foil and chill overnight. Slice cookies 3/8 in. thick.

- Bake on greased baking sheets at 350° for about 10 minutes.

YIELD: ABOUT 17 DOZEN.

AUNT IONE'S ICEBOX COOKIES

CRAN-ORANGE ICEBOX COOKIES

cran-orange icebox cookies

PREP 30 min. + chilling
BAKE 10 min.

NANCY ROLLAG • KEWASKUM, WISCONSIN

These cookies are a favorite with my clan, especially at Christmas. The refreshing cran-orange flavor is a nice departure from typical butter cookies.

- 1 cup butter, softened
- 1 cup sugar
- 1 egg
- 2 tablespoons 2% milk
- 1 teaspoon vanilla extract
- 3 cups all-purpose flour
- 1-1/2 teaspoons baking powder
- 2 teaspoons grated orange peel
- 2/3 cup chopped dried cranberries
- 1/4 cup chopped pecans
- 8 to 10 drops red food coloring, optional

- In a large bowl, cream butter and sugar until light and fluffy. Beat in the egg, milk and vanilla. Combine flour and baking powder; gradually add to creamed mixture and mix well.

- Transfer 1 cup of dough to a small bowl; stir in orange peel and set aside. Add the cranberries, pecans and food coloring if desired to remaining dough; divide in half.

- Line an 8-in. x 4-in. loaf pan with waxed paper. Press one portion of cranberry dough evenly into pan; top with orange dough, then remaining cranberry dough. Cover and refrigerate for 2 hours or until firm.

- Remove dough from pan; cut in half lengthwise. Cut each portion into 1/4-in. slices. Place 1 in. apart on lightly greased baking sheets.

- Bake at 375° for 8-10 minutes or until edges begin to brown. Remove to wire racks. Store in an airtight container.

YIELD: 4 DOZEN.

CHERRY-ORANGE ICEBOX COOKIES: Substitute dried cherries for the cranberries and almonds for the pecans.

tip

easy slicing

Use dental floss to easily slice refrigerator cookie dough. Place a piece of floss (about 1 foot long) under the roll of dough, crisscross the ends above the dough and pull until you've cut through to make a slice.

jeweled cookies

PREP 15 min. + freezing
BAKE 10 min.

RUTH ANN STELFOX • RAYMOND, ALBERTA

Candied fruits give a stained-glass look to these shortbread cookies. They make a colorful addition to holiday cookie platters.

- 1 pound butter, softened
- 2-1/2 cups sugar
- 3 eggs
- 5 cups all-purpose flour
- 1 teaspoon baking soda
- 1-1/2 cups raisins
- 1 cup coarsely chopped walnuts
- 1/2 cup *each* chopped red and green candied cherries
- 1/2 cup chopped candied pineapple

• In a bowl, cream butter and sugar. Add eggs, one at a time, beating well after each. Combine flour and baking soda; add to creamed mixture. Stir in raisins, nuts, cherries and pineapple; mix well. Shape into 2-in. rolls; wrap in waxed paper or foil. Freeze at least 2 hours.

• Cut into 1/4-in. slices; place on greased baking sheets. Bake at 350° for 8-10 minutes or until lightly browned. Cool on wire racks.

YIELD: 12-14 DOZEN.

chocolate monster cookies

PREP 20 min. + chilling
BAKE 15 min.

HELEN HILBERT • LIVERPOOL, NEW YORK

Little cooks can have fun stirring in all the added ingredients to the batter in this recipe. I recommend using an extra-large bowl to prevent spillage.

- 2 cups butter, softened
- 2 cups sugar
- 2 cups packed brown sugar
- 4 eggs
- 2 teaspoons vanilla extract
- 4 cups all-purpose flour
- 3 teaspoons baking powder
- 2 teaspoons baking soda
- 1 teaspoon salt
- 2 cups cornflakes
- 2 cups rolled oats
- 1 package (8 ounces) flaked coconut

- 1 package (12 ounces) semisweet chocolate chips
- 1 cup chopped walnuts

• In a large bowl, cream butter and sugars. Beat in eggs and vanilla. Combine the flour, baking powder, baking soda and salt; gradually add to creamed mixture and mix well. Stir in the cornflakes, oats and coconut. (It may be necessary to transfer to a larger bowl to stir in the cornflakes, oats and coconut.) Stir in chocolate chips and nuts.

• Divide dough into six sections. Shape each into a 7-in. x 1-1/2-in. roll. Wrap each in plastic wrap. Refrigerate several hours or overnight.

• Unwrap dough; cut into 1/2-in. slices. Place 3 in. apart on ungreased baking sheets. Bake at 350° for 13-15 minutes or until edges are browned. Remove to wire racks to cool.

YIELD: 7-1/2 DOZEN.

fudgy pinwheel cookies

PREP 25 min. + chilling
BAKE 10 min.

MAUREEN DEVLIN • CHANDLER, ARIZONA

These quick and easy cookies are one of my all-time favorites. No one can resist their fudgy taste.

- 1/2 cup butter, softened
- 1/2 cup packed brown sugar
- 1 egg yolk
- 1/2 teaspoon vanilla extract
- 1 cup all-purpose flour
- 1/2 teaspoon salt
- 1/4 teaspoon baking powder

FILLING:

- 1 cup (6 ounces) semisweet chocolate chips
- 1 tablespoon shortening
- 1 cup finely chopped walnuts
- 1/3 cup sweetened condensed milk
- 1 teaspoon vanilla extract

• In a large bowl, cream butter and brown sugar until light and fluffy. Beat in egg yolk and vanilla. Combine the flour, salt and baking powder; gradually add to creamed mixture and mix well.

• Roll out dough into a 12-in. x 10-in. rectangle between two sheets of waxed paper; transfer to a baking sheet. Refrigerate for 30 minutes.

• In a small microwave-safe bowl, melt the chocolate chips and shortening. Stir in the walnuts, milk and vanilla. Remove the waxed paper from dough; spread with filling. Tightly roll up jelly-roll style, starting with a long side. Wrap in plastic wrap; refrigerate for 2 hours or until firm.

• Unwrap and cut into 1/4-in. slices. Place 2 in. apart on lightly greased baking sheets. Bake at 375° for 8-10 minutes or until set. Remove to wire racks. Store in an airtight container.

YIELD: ABOUT 2-1/2 DOZEN.

FUDGY PINWHEEL COOKIES

DATE PINWHEELS

date pinwheels

PREP 45 min. + chilling
BAKE 10 min.

LEE ROBERTS • RACINE, WISCONSIN

This is a great recipe for a delicious pinwheel to serve at the end of any meal. The dates add a unique taste that makes these stand apart.

- 1 cup butter, softened
- 2 cups packed brown sugar
- 3 eggs
- 1 teaspoon vanilla extract
- 4 cups all-purpose flour
- 1/2 teaspoon salt
- 1/2 teaspoon baking soda

FILLING:

- 2-1/2 cups chopped dates
- 1 cup sugar
- 1 cup water
- 1 cup finely chopped pecans

● In a large bowl, cream butter and brown sugar until light and fluffy. Beat in eggs and vanilla. Combine the flour, salt and baking soda; gradually add to creamed mixture and mix well. Divide into four portions. Refrigerate until chilled.

● In a large saucepan, bring the dates, sugar and water to a boil. Reduce heat to medium; cook until mixture is thickened, about 15 minutes. Cool completely. Stir in pecans.

● On a baking sheet, roll out each portion of dough between two sheets of waxed paper into a 12-in. x 9-in. rectangle. Refrigerate for 30 minutes.

● Remove waxed paper; spread with the date mixture. Tightly roll up each portion jelly-roll style, starting with a long side; wrap in plastic wrap. Refrigerate for 2 hours or until firm.

● Unwrap and cut into 1/4-in. slices. Place 1 in. apart on greased baking sheets. Bake at 350° for 10-12 minutes or until set. Remove to wire racks to cool. Store cookies in an airtight container at room temperature, or freeze for up to 3 months.

YIELD: 16 DOZEN.

icebox spice cookies

PREP 45 min. + chilling
BAKE 10 min.

CAROLINE SMID • WINNIPEG, MANITOBA

These slice-and-bake cookies become very crispy after they've cooled. They're wonderful dunked in a cup of coffee or a glass of milk.

- 1-1/4 cups butter, softened
- 1 cup sugar
- 1 cup packed brown sugar
- 2 eggs
- 3-3/4 cups all-purpose flour
- 2 teaspoons ground cinnamon
- 1 teaspoon baking soda
- 1 teaspoon salt
- 1 teaspoon ground cloves
- 1 teaspoon ground allspice

● In a large bowl, cream butter and sugars until light and fluffy. Add eggs, one at a time, beating well after each addition. Combine the flour, cinnamon, baking soda, salt, cloves and allspice; gradually add to creamed mixture and mix well.

● Shape into three 6-in. rolls; wrap each in plastic wrap. Refrigerate for at least 2 hours or until firm.

● Unwrap dough and cut into 1/4-in. slices. Place 2 in. apart on greased baking sheets. Bake at 350° for 8-10 minutes or until lightly browned around the edges. Cool for 1-2 minutes before removing to wire racks.

YIELD: 6 DOZEN.

crisp lemon tea cookies

PREP 40 min. + chilling
BAKE 10 min. + cooling

TASTE OF HOME TEST KITCHEN

These lemony cookies make the perfect backdrop for an assortment of colorful baking bits, sprinkles or edible glitter. They're almost as much fun to decorate as they are to eat!

- 1/2 cup butter, softened
- 1/2 cup sugar
- 1 tablespoon 2% milk
- 1/2 teaspoon vanilla extract
- 1-1/4 cups all-purpose flour
- 1/2 teaspoon ground cinnamon

FROSTING:

- 2 tablespoons plus 1 teaspoon butter
- 1-1/2 cups confectioners' sugar
- 2 tablespoons lemon juice

Assorted M&M's miniature baking bits

● In a small bowl, cream butter and sugar until light and fluffy. Beat in milk and vanilla. Gradually add flour and cinnamon to creamed mixture. Shape dough into an 8-in. x 2-in. roll; wrap in plastic wrap and freeze.

● TO USE FROZEN COOKIE DOUGH: Unwrap dough and let stand at room temperature for 10 minutes. Cut into 1/4-in. slices. Place 2 in. apart on ungreased baking sheets. Bake at 375° for 8-10 minutes or until lightly browned. Remove to wire racks to cool.

● For frosting, in another small bowl, cream the butter and confectioners' sugar. Gradually beat in lemon juice. Frost cookies. Decorate with baking bits.

YIELD: 2 DOZEN.

EDITOR'S NOTE: This recipe does not use eggs.

pot o' gold cookies

PREP 20 min. + chilling
BAKE 15 min. + cooling

KERRY BARNETT-AMUNDSON
OCEAN PARK, WASHINGTON

These soft, buttery delights are always a hit, plus you can flavor the dough any way you like. I've used chopped pecans, walnuts... even maraschino cherries.

- 1 cup butter, softened
- 1/2 cup sugar
- 1 tablespoon 2% milk
- 1/2 teaspoon vanilla extract
- 1/8 teaspoon almond extract
- 2 cups all-purpose flour
- 1/2 cup finely chopped almonds, toasted

Dash salt

ICING:

- 2 cups confectioners' sugar
- 2 tablespoons plus 2 teaspoons 2% milk

Green food coloring

- In a large bowl, cream butter and sugar until light and fluffy. Beat in milk and extracts.

- Combine the flour, almonds and salt; gradually add to the creamed mixture and mix well. Shape dough into a 10-in. roll; wrap in plastic wrap. Refrigerate overnight.

- Unwrap and cut into 1/4-in. slices. Place 2 in. apart on ungreased baking sheets. Bake at 325° for 14-16 minutes or until set. Remove to wire racks to cool.

- Combine the icing ingredients; decorate the cookies as desired. Let stand until set. Store in an airtight container.

YIELD: ABOUT 3-1/2 DOZEN.

almond-edged butter cookies

PREP 20 min. + chilling
BAKE 10 min.

DIANE NELSON • APPLE VALLEY, CALIFORNIA

I know you will love these cookies because everyone who's tried them can't get enough! The light, crunchy texture melts in your mouth.

- 1 cup butter, softened
- 1-1/3 cups plus 6 tablespoons sugar, *divided*
- 2 eggs, *separated*
- 1/4 cup half-and-half cream
- 1 teaspoon vanilla extract
- 3 cups all-purpose flour
- 2 teaspoons baking powder
- 1/2 teaspoon salt
- 1 cup sliced almonds, toasted and chopped

- In a large bowl, cream butter and 1-1/3 cups sugar until light and fluffy. Beat in the egg yolks, cream and vanilla. Combine the flour, baking powder and salt; gradually add to creamed mixture and mix well.

- Shape into four 1-1/2-in. rolls; wrap each roll in plastic wrap. Refrigerate dough for 1 hour or until firm.

- In a shallow bowl, combine almonds and remaining sugar. In a small bowl, lightly beat egg whites. Unwrap dough; brush with egg whites. Roll in almond mixture, pressing firmly into dough. Cut into 1/4-in. slices.

- Place 2 in. apart on lightly greased baking sheets. Bake at 400° for 7-8 minutes or until edges are lightly browned. Remove to wire racks. Store in an airtight container.

YIELD: ABOUT 7-1/2 DOZEN.

RIBBON ICEBOX COOKIES

ribbon icebox cookies

PREP 25 min. + chilling
BAKE 10 min.

KARLYNE MOREAU • YAKIMA, WASHINGTON

Three ribbons of flavor—cherry, chocolate and poppy seed—combine to create one tender, Neapolitan-style cookie.

- 1/2 cup shortening
- 2/3 cup sugar
- 2 tablespoons beaten egg
- 1/2 teaspoon vanilla extract
- 1-1/4 cups all-purpose flour
- 3/4 teaspoon baking powder
- 1/4 teaspoon salt
- 2 tablespoons red candied cherries, chopped
- 1/2 ounce unsweetened chocolate, melted
- 2 teaspoons poppy seeds

- Line a 5-in. x 3-in. x 2-in. loaf pan with waxed paper; set aside. In a small bowl, cream shortening and sugar until light and fluffy. Beat in egg and vanilla. Combine the flour, baking powder and salt; gradually add to creamed mixture and mix well.

- Divide dough into thirds. Add the cherries to one portion; spread evenly into prepared pan. Add the melted chocolate to second portion; spread evenly over first layer. Add poppy seeds to third portion; spread over second layer. Cover with waxed paper; refrigerate overnight.

- Unwrap the dough and cut into 1/4-in. slices. Place 1 in. apart on ungreased baking sheets. Bake at 375° for 8-9 minutes or until lightly browned. Cool for 1 minute before removing to wire racks.

YIELD: ABOUT 1-1/2 DOZEN.

POT O' GOLD COOKIES

shaped cookies

Have fun shaping dough into balls, crescents, cups and other fanciful cookie creations with the delightful recipes offered here.

PICTURED ABOVE: CHOCOLATE-DIPPED COCONUT SNOWBALLS, PAGE 46 • BRANDY SNAP CANNOLI, PAGE 42
CHOCOLATE CAKE COOKIES, PAGE 51 • NO-BAKE ALMOND BITES, PAGE 41

FRUIT-FILLED DAINTIES

walnut horn cookies

PREP 40 min.
BAKE 35 min.

LORETTA STOKES
PHILADELPHIA, PENNSYLVANIA

It only takes a few ingredients to create these elegant and delicious walnut horns. This is a great recipe for time-pressed cooks as the dough can be made in advance and refrigerated for 5 to 7 days.

    1 cup plus 1 teaspoon butter, softened, *divided*
    1 package (8 ounces) cream cheese, softened
    3 cups all-purpose flour
    4 cups ground walnuts
1-1/4 cups sugar, *divided*
  1/2 cup 2% milk
    1 teaspoon vanilla extract
  1/8 teaspoon salt

- In a large bowl, beat 1 cup butter and the cream cheese until light and fluffy. Gradually add flour, beating until mixture forms a ball. Divide dough into four portions; roll each into a 12-in. circle.

- Melt the remaining butter. In a large bowl, combine the walnuts, 3/4 cup sugar, milk, vanilla, salt and melted butter. Spread over the circles. Cut each into 12 wedges. Roll up wedges, starting from the wide ends.

- Place cookies point side down on greased baking sheets. Curve ends to form crescents. Bake at 325° for 35-40 minutes or until lightly browned. Remove to wire racks.

- Place the remaining sugar in a small shallow bowl. Roll warm cookies in sugar.

YIELD: 4 DOZEN.

WALNUT HORN COOKIES

fruit-filled dainties

PREP 25 min.
BAKE 10 min.

TASTE OF HOME TEST KITCHEN

With this easy recipe you can shape convenient refrigerated dough into cookies or tarts. Use one filling or make them both.

CRAN-ORANGE FILLING:

    2 cups dried cranberries
    9 tablespoons orange marmalade

APRICOT-ORANGE FILLING:

    9 tablespoons orange marmalade
4-1/2 teaspoons water
2-1/4 cups chopped dried apricots

DOUGH:

    1 tube (18 ounces) refrigerated sugar cookie dough, softened
  1/4 cup all-purpose flour
Confectioners' sugar

- Prepare either the cran-orange or apricot-orange filling. For cran-orange filling, combine cranberries and marmalade in a food processor; cover and process until finely chopped. For apricot-orange filling, combine the marmalade, water and apricots in a food processor; cover and process until finely chopped.

- In a large bowl, beat cookie dough and flour until smooth. Divide into thirds. Work with one portion at a time and keep remaining dough covered.

- TO PREPARE COOKIES: On a floured surface, roll out one portion of dough to 1/8-in. thickness. Cut into 2-1/2-in. squares or cut with a 2-1/2-in. round cookie cutter. Place 1 in. apart on ungreased baking sheets. Repeat with remaining dough.

- Place a slightly rounded teaspoon of filling in the center of each square or circle. Shape by folding two opposite points of squares over one another or by folding edges of circles together; press to seal. Bake at 350° for 9-12 minutes or until lightly browned. Cool for 2 minutes before removing to wire racks. Dust with confectioners' sugar.

- TO PREPARE TARTS: Shape one portion of dough into twelve 1-in. balls. Press onto the bottom and up the sides of ungreased miniature muffin cups. Repeat with remaining dough. Bake at 350° for 10-12 minutes or until lightly browned.

- Using the end of a wooden spoon handle, gently make a 3/8- to 1/2-in.-deep indentation in the center of each tart. Cool for 10 minutes before removing from pans to wire racks. Dust with confectioners' sugar. Spoon about a tablespoon of filling into each tart.

YIELD: 3 DOZEN.

EDITOR'S NOTE: Each type of filling makes enough to yield three dozen cookies. If you would like to use both fillings, make two batches of the dough.

dipped vanillas

PREP 30 min. + chilling
BAKE 10 min. + chilling

KAREN BOURNE • MAGRATH, ALBERTA

A touch of chocolate makes these classics stand out on a cookie tray. They're a tradition at our home for the holidays.

1/2	cup butter, softened
1/2	cup ground almonds
1/4	cup sugar
1	teaspoon vanilla extract
1	cup all-purpose flour
2	tablespoons cornstarch
2	ounces semisweet chocolate
1/2	teaspoon shortening

• In a small bowl, beat the butter, almonds, sugar and vanilla until blended. Gradually add flour and cornstarch; mix well. Roll into 1-in. balls; shape into crescents and place on greased baking sheets.

• Bake at 375° for 8-10 minutes or until lightly browned. Cool completely on wire racks.

• Melt chocolate and shortening in a microwave; stir until smooth. Dip one end of each crescent into chocolate; decorate as desired. Place on waxed paper-lined baking sheets. Refrigerate for 30 minutes or until set.

YIELD: ABOUT 2-1/2 DOZEN.

CARAMEL PECAN TREASURES

DIPPED VANILLAS

caramel pecan treasures

PREP 25 min. + standing
BAKE 15 min. + cooling

GLENDA MACEACHERN • CROWN POINT, INDIANA

Fancy sensations like these may take some time to prepare, but family and friends will surely be impressed! No one can resist the shortbread cookie, caramel filling and melted chocolate top sprinkled with pecans.

1	cup butter, softened
3/4	cup packed brown sugar
1	teaspoon vanilla extract
1-3/4	cups all-purpose flour
1/2	teaspoon baking powder
30	caramels, halved and flattened
2	cups (12 ounces) semisweet chocolate chips
1	tablespoon shortening
1/2	cup finely chopped pecans

• In a large bowl, cream butter and brown sugar until light and fluffy. Beat in vanilla. Combine flour and baking powder; gradually add to creamed mixture and mix well.

• Roll dough into 1-in. balls. Place 2 in. apart on greased baking sheets; flatten slightly. Bake at 325° for 12-15 minutes or until golden brown. Remove to wire racks to cool.

• Place a half-caramel on each cookie. Melt the chocolate chips and shortening; drizzle over cookies. Sprinkle with pecans. Let stand until firm.

YIELD: 5 DOZEN.

chocolate puddles

PREP 25 min. + chilling
BAKE 10 min.

KATHIE GRIFFIN • ANTELOPE, CALIFORNIA

The variations on this fantastic recipe are almost endless. For double chocolate puddles, use semisweet chocolate chips for the vanilla chips. Or make peanut butter puddles by substituting peanut butter chips and peanuts for the vanilla chips and mixed nuts.

1	cup butter, softened
1	cup sugar
1	cup packed brown sugar
2	eggs
2	teaspoons vanilla extract
3	cups all-purpose flour
3/4	cup baking cocoa
1	teaspoon baking soda

FILLING:

- 1 cup white baking chips
- 1/2 cup plus 2 tablespoons sweetened condensed milk
- 3/4 cup finely chopped mixed nuts

• In a large bowl, cream butter and sugars until light and fluffy. Add the eggs, one at a time, beating well after each addition. Beat in vanilla. Combine the flour, cocoa and baking soda; gradually add to the creamed mixture and mix well. Cover and refrigerate for 2 hours or until dough is stiff.

• Meanwhile, for filling, heat chips and milk in a heavy saucepan over low heat until chips are melted, stirring constantly. Stir in nuts. Cover and refrigerate for 1 hour or until easy to handle.

• Roll cookie dough into 1-1/4-in. balls. Place 2 in. apart on lightly greased baking sheets. Using the end of a wooden spoon handle, make an indentation in the center; smooth any cracks.

• Roll filling into 1/2-in. balls; gently push one into each cookie. Bake at 375° for 8-10 minutes or until cookies are set. Remove to wire racks to cool.

YIELD: ABOUT 5 DOZEN.

decorated butter cookies

PREP 20 min.
BAKE 10 min.

DORIS SCHUMACHER
BROOKINGS, SOUTH DAKOTA

Tender, crisp and flavorful, these versatile cookies can be decorated to suit any season or occasion. Or simply lightly frost and sprinkle with toasted coconut flakes.

- 1 cup butter, softened
- 1/2 cup sugar
- 1/2 cup packed brown sugar
- 1 egg
- 1 teaspoon vanilla extract
- 2 cups all-purpose flour
- 2 teaspoons cream of tartar
- 1 teaspoon baking soda
- 1/8 teaspoon salt
Colored sprinkles, colored sugar, ground nuts *and/or* chocolate sprinkles

• In a small bowl, cream butter and sugars until light and fluffy. Beat in egg and vanilla. Combine the flour, cream of tartar, baking soda and salt;

gradually add to creamed mixture and mix well. Cover and refrigerate for 1 hour or until easy to handle.

• Roll into 1-in. balls. Place 2 in. apart on ungreased baking sheets. Flatten with a glass dipped in sugar; sprinkle with sprinkles, colored sugar or nuts.

• Bake at 350° for 10-12 minutes or until lightly browned. Remove to wire racks to cool.

YIELD: 4 DOZEN.

raspberry coconut cookies

PREP 30 min.
BAKE 10 min.

CHERYL GIROUX • AMHERSTBURG, ONTARIO

These chewy treats with smooth raspberry centers will disappear fast. My mom made these delights when I was growing up, and now I make them for my gang. Store cooled cookies in a sealed container to keep them soft.

- 1/2 cup shortening
- 1/2 cup packed brown sugar
- 6 tablespoons sugar
- 1 egg
- 1/4 cup water
- 1/2 teaspoon almond extract
- 1-1/2 cups plus 2 tablespoons all-purpose flour
- 1/2 teaspoon salt
- 1/2 teaspoon baking soda
- 1 cup flaked coconut
- 1/3 cup seedless raspberry jam

• In a large bowl, cream shortening and sugars until light and fluffy. Beat in the egg, water and extract. Combine the flour, salt and baking soda; gradually add to creamed mixture and mix well. Stir in coconut (dough will be sticky).

• Set aside 2/3 cup dough; roll the remaining dough into 1-in. balls. Using the end of a wooden spoon handle, make a 3/8-in. deep indentation in the center of each ball. Fill each with 1/2 teaspoon jam. Cover jam with a teaspoonful of reserved dough; seal and reshape into a ball. Repeat.

• Place 2 in. apart on ungreased baking sheets. Bake at 375° for 10-12 minutes or until lightly browned. Remove to wire racks to cool.

YIELD: ABOUT 2-1/2 DOZEN.

RASPBERRY COCONUT COOKIES

SMILING SUGAR COOKIES

smiling sugar cookies

PREP 30 min.
BAKE 10 min. + standing

BRENDA BAWDON • ALPENA, SOUTH DAKOTA

These cute cookie pops are a big hit at bake sales. I sell them for $1 a piece and watch them disappear! The bright and cheery faces always catch kids' eyes.

- 1/2 cup butter, softened
- 1/2 cup sugar
- 1/2 cup packed brown sugar
- 1 egg
- 1/3 cup 2% milk
- 2 teaspoons vanilla extract
- 3 cups all-purpose flour
- 2 teaspoons cream of tartar
- 1 teaspoon baking soda
- 1/2 teaspoon salt
- About 24 Popsicle sticks
- 1 cup vanilla frosting
- Red, blue and green paste food coloring
- Assorted small candies

- In a large bowl, cream the butter and sugars until light and fluffy. Beat in the egg, milk and vanilla. Combine the flour, cream of tartar, baking soda and salt; gradually add to creamed mixture and mix well. Roll dough into 1-1/2-in. balls; insert a Popsicle stick in the center of each ball.

- Place 2 in. apart on lightly greased baking sheets; flatten slightly. Bake at 375° for 8-10 minutes or until lightly browned. Remove to wire racks to cool.

- Divide frosting among three bowls; tint as desired. Place each color of frosting in a resealable plastic bag; cut a small hole in a corner of bag. Pipe hair and mouths onto cookies; use a dab of frosting to attach small candies for eyes. Let dry for at least 30 minutes.

YIELD: ABOUT 2 DOZEN.

peanut butter cup cookies

PREP 20 min. + chilling
BAKE 15 min.

MARY HEPPERLE • TORONTO, ONTARIO

The first time I made these, I got so many requests for the recipe that I knew I had a hit!

- 1 cup butter, softened
- 1/2 cup creamy peanut butter
- 3/4 cup packed brown sugar
- 1/2 cup sugar
- 1 egg
- 1 teaspoon vanilla extract
- 2 cups all-purpose flour
- 1 teaspoon baking soda
- 1 package (13 ounces) miniature peanut butter cups

DRIZZLE:
- 1 cup (6 ounces) semisweet chocolate chips
- 1 tablespoon creamy peanut butter
- 1 teaspoon shortening

- In a large bowl, cream the butter, peanut butter and sugars until light and fluffy. Beat in egg and vanilla. Combine flour and baking soda; gradually add to creamed mixture and mix well. Cover and refrigerate for 1 hour or until easy to handle.

- Roll into 1-1/4-in. balls. Press a miniature peanut butter cup into each; reshape balls. Place 2 in. apart on ungreased baking sheets.

- Bake at 350° for 12-15 minutes or until edges are lightly browned. Cool for 2 minutes before removing from pans to wire racks.

- For drizzle, in a microwave, melt the chocolate chips, peanut butter and shortening; stir until smooth. Drizzle over cooled cookies.

YIELD: ABOUT 3 DOZEN.

EDITOR'S NOTE: Reduced-fat or generic brands of peanut butter are not recommended for this recipe.

tip

homemade p.b. cups

It's easy to make homemade peanut butter cups. In a microwave, melt 2 cups chocolate chips and 2 tablespoons shortening; stir until smooth. Place a scant teaspoonful inside mini foil cups and rotate it gently in the palm of your hand to coat the sides and bottom. Place cups in miniature muffin pans; chill until firm. Set remaining chocolate aside. In a medium bowl, combine 1 cup peanut butter, 1/2 cup nonfat dry milk powder, 1/2 cup light corn syrup and 1 teaspoon vanilla extract until smooth. Shape into 1-in. balls; press a ball into each chocolate cup. Top with remaining melted chocolate. Chill until set. Store in an airtight container in the refrigerator.

no-bake almond bites

PREP 10 min.

TASTE OF HOME TEST KITCHEN

To help keep snacking on the skinny side, our Test Kitchen experts whipped up these little sensations that have only 81 calories per serving. Quick and easy, the chewy no-bake treats are ideal when time is tight.

- 1 cup crushed reduced-fat vanilla wafers (about 30 wafers)
- 1 cup confectioners' sugar, *divided*
- 1/2 cup chopped almonds
- 2 tablespoons baking cocoa
- 2 tablespoons apple juice
- 2 tablespoons corn syrup
- 1/4 teaspoon almond extract

• In a large bowl, combine the wafer crumbs, 1/2 cup confectioners' sugar, almonds and cocoa. Combine the apple juice, corn syrup and extract; stir into crumb mixture until blended.

• Shape into 1-in. balls; roll in the remaining confectioners' sugar. Store the cookies in an airtight container.

YIELD: 1-1/2 DOZEN.

pistachio chip cookies

PREP 20 min.
BAKE 10 min.

MALINDA MOORE DAVIES
FRESNO, CALIFORNIA

Coming from a family of pistachio producers, I've collected hundreds of recipes featuring these delicious green nuts. This one is a favorite.

- 1-1/4 cups butter, softened
- 2 cups packed brown sugar
- 2 eggs
- 2 teaspoons vanilla extract
- 2-1/2 cups all-purpose flour
- 1 teaspoon baking powder
- 1 teaspoon baking soda
- 1/2 cup old-fashioned oats
- 1 package (12 ounces) white baking chips
- 1-1/3 cups chopped pistachios, *divided*

• In a bowl, cream butter and sugar. Add eggs and vanilla; mix well. Combine flour, baking powder, baking soda and oats; gradually add to creamed mixture and mix well. Stir in chips and 1 cup pistachios.

NO-BAKE ALMOND BITES

MERINGUE DROPS

• Shape into 1-in. balls; place 2 in. apart on ungreased baking sheets. Lightly press remaining pistachios into cookies.

• Bake at 350° for 10-12 minutes or until lightly browned. Cool 2 minutes before removing to wire racks.

YIELD: ABOUT 9 DOZEN.

meringue drops

PREP 25 min.
BAKE 20 min. + cooling

TASTE OF HOME TEST KITCHEN

These pretty pastel cookies are a fun way to brighten a springtime luncheon, baby shower or any special occasion. If you don't have time to pipe the meringue, simply spoon it into 2-in. circles. Replace the vanilla with a different extract for a change of flavor.

- 3 egg whites
- 1/2 teaspoon vanilla extract
- 1/4 teaspoon cream of tartar
- Food coloring, optional
- 3/4 cup sugar
- White pearl *or* coarse sugar, optional

• Place egg whites in a large bowl; let stand at room temperature for 30 minutes. Add vanilla, cream of tartar and food coloring if desired; beat on medium speed until soft peaks form. Gradually beat in sugar, 1 tablespoon at a time, on high until stiff peaks form.

• Cut a small hole in the corner of a pastry or plastic bag; insert #3 star pastry tip. Fill bag with meringue. Pipe 2-in. circles or shapes 2 in. apart onto parchment paper-lined baking sheets. Sprinkle with pearl sugar if desired.

• Bake at 300° for 20-25 minutes or until set and dry. Turn oven off; leave meringues in oven for 1 hour. Store in an airtight container.

YIELD: ABOUT 2 DOZEN.

LARA'S TENDER GINGERSNAPS

lara's tender gingersnaps

PREP 15 min. + chilling
BAKE 10 min.

LARA PENNELL • MAULDIN, SOUTH CAROLINA

Soft gingersnaps embody the flavors and aromas of the season. Perfect for fall gatherings, these gems let you enjoy cloves, cinnamon and ginger blended into one unique, delicious cookie.

    1   cup packed brown sugar
    3/4   cup butter, melted
    1   egg
    1/4   cup molasses
    2-1/4 cups all-purpose flour
    1-1/2 teaspoons ground ginger
    1   teaspoon baking soda
    1   teaspoon ground cinnamon
    1/2   teaspoon ground cloves
    1/4   cup sugar

• In a large bowl, beat brown sugar and butter until blended. Beat in egg, then molasses. Combine the flour, ginger, baking soda, cinnamon and cloves; gradually add to brown sugar mixture and mix well (dough will be stiff). Cover and refrigerate for at least 2 hours.

• Shape dough into 1 in. balls. Roll in sugar. Place 2 in. apart on baking sheets coated with cooking spray. Bake at 350° for 9-11 minutes or until set. Cool for 1 minute before removing from pans to wire racks.

YIELD: 3 DOZEN.

brandy snap cannoli

PREP 1-1/2 hours
BAKE 5 min. + cooling

TASTE OF HOME TEST KITCHEN

This recipe combines two all-time classics...brandy snaps and cannoli. You can assemble and chill them an hour before serving.

    1/2   cup butter, cubed
    1/2   cup sugar
    3   tablespoons molasses
    1   teaspoon ground ginger
    1/4   teaspoon salt
    1   cup all-purpose flour
    2   tablespoons brandy

FILLING:

    1-1/2 cups ricotta cheese
    3   tablespoons grated orange peel
    3   tablespoons sugar, *divided*
    1-1/2 cups miniature semisweet
          chocolate chips, *divided*
    1-1/2 cups heavy whipping cream

• In a small saucepan, combine the first five ingredients. Cook and stir over medium heat until butter is melted. Remove from the heat. Stir in flour and brandy; keep warm.

• Drop the batter by tablespoonfuls onto a parchment paper-lined or well-greased baking sheet; spread each into a 4-in. circle. Bake at 350° for 5-6 minutes or until edges begin to brown. Cool for about 1 minute or just until cookie starts to firm.

• Working quickly, loosen each cookie and curl around a metal cannoli tube to shape. Remove cookies from tubes; cool on wire racks.

• For filling, in a large bowl, combine the ricotta, orange peel and 1 tablespoon sugar; stir in 1/2 cup chocolate chips. In a small bowl, beat cream on medium speed until soft peaks form. Gradually add remaining sugar, beating on high until stiff peaks form. Fold into ricotta mixture. Chill until serving.

• Just before serving, pipe filling into cannoli shells. Dip ends in remaining chocolate chips.

YIELD: ABOUT 2 DOZEN.

glazed italian spice cookies

PREP 40 min.
BAKE 10 min. + cooling

SHELIA HAKE • BOSSIER CITY, LOUISIANA

These cute little balls are a tender, cake-like option for your dessert tray. The creamy almond glaze spread on top makes these bites extra yummy.

    1   cup shortening
    1-1/4 cups sugar
    3   eggs
    1   cup milk
    5   cups all-purpose flour

BRANDY SNAP CANNOLI

1/4 cup plus 3 tablespoons baking cocoa

5 teaspoons baking powder

1 teaspoon ground cinnamon

1 teaspoon ground nutmeg

1/2 teaspoon ground cloves

1/4 teaspoon baking soda

1 cup finely chopped pecans

GLAZE:

6 tablespoons butter, softened

2-1/2 cups confectioners' sugar

3 tablespoons milk

1 teaspoon vanilla extract

1/4 teaspoon almond extract

- In a large bowl, cream shortening and sugar until light and fluffy. Beat in eggs and milk. Combine the flour, cocoa, baking powder, cinnamon, nutmeg, cloves and baking soda; gradually add to creamed mixture and mix well. Stir in pecans.

- Roll dough into 1-in. balls. Place 1 in. apart on greased baking sheets. Bake at 350° for 9-11 minutes or until edges are set. Remove to wire racks to cool.

- For glaze, in a large bowl, beat the butter until fluffy. Add the confectioners' sugar, milk, and extracts; beat until smooth. Spread over cooled cookies.

YIELD: 7-1/2 DOZEN.

WHITE CHOCOLATE NUT CRACKLES

strawberry cream cookies

PREP 25 min. + chilling
BAKE 10 min.

GLENNA ABERLE • SABETHA, KANSAS

These delicate cream cheese sensations look so lovely on a tea tray or dessert platter. Feel free to try other jam flavors such as apricot, raspberry or blueberry.

1 cup butter, softened

1 package (3 ounces) cream cheese, softened

1 cup sugar

1 egg yolk

3 teaspoons vanilla extract

2-1/2 cups all-purpose flour

Seedless strawberry jam

- In a large bowl, cream the butter, cream cheese and sugar until light and fluffy. Beat in egg yolk and vanilla. Add flour and mix well. Cover and refrigerate for 1 hour or until easy to handle.

- Shape dough into 1-in. balls. Place 2 in. apart on ungreased baking sheets. Using the end of a wooden spoon handle, make a 1/2-in.-deep indentation in the center of each ball; fill with about 1/4 teaspoon jam. Bake cookies at 350° for 10-12 minutes or until set. Remove to wire racks to cool.

YIELD: 5 DOZEN.

white chocolate nut crackles

PREP 25 min. + chilling
BAKE 10 min.

JOYCE GETHING • PAMPA, TEXAS

My aunt and I would bake together when I was growing up, and we had a similar recipe for a white cookie. After some experimentation, I added the macadamia nuts and white chocolate chips. My family and coworkers rave over these delights.

1/2 cup butter, softened

1/2 cup shortening

1/2 cup sugar

1/2 cup packed brown sugar

1 egg

1 teaspoon vanilla extract

2 cups all-purpose flour

1 teaspoon baking soda

1 teaspoon cream of tartar

1/2 teaspoon salt

6 ounces white baking chocolate, coarsely chopped

1/2 cup coarsely chopped macadamia nuts, toasted

Additional sugar

- In a large bowl, cream the butter, shortening and sugars until light and fluffy. Beat in egg and vanilla. Combine the flour, baking soda, cream of tartar and salt; gradually add to the creamed mixture and mix well. Stir in chocolate and nuts. Cover and refrigerate for 1 hour or until easy to handle.

- Roll dough into 1-in. balls. Dip each ball halfway in water, then in sugar. Place sugar side up 2 in. apart on ungreased baking sheets; flatten slightly.

- Bake at 400° for 8-10 minutes or until golden brown. Remove to wire racks to cool.

YIELD: 5-1/2 DOZEN.

1 cup butter, softened
1 cup confectioners' sugar
2 teaspoons vanilla extract
2 cups all-purpose flour
1 teaspoon salt

TOPPING:

1 package (3 ounces) cream cheese, softened
1 cup confectioners' sugar
2 tablespoons all-purpose flour
1 teaspoon vanilla extract
1/2 cup flaked coconut
1/2 cup finely chopped walnuts
3/4 cup semisweet chocolate chips, melted

- In a large bowl, cream butter and confectioners' sugar until light and fluffy. Beat in vanilla. Combine flour and salt; gradually add to creamed mixture and mix well.

- Shape into 1-in. balls. Place 2 in. apart on ungreased baking sheets. Using the end of a wooden spoon handle, make a 1/2-in.-deep indentation in the center of each ball.

- Bake at 350° for 10-12 minutes or until lightly browned. Remove to wire racks to cool.

- For filling, in a small bowl, beat the cream cheese and confectioners' sugar until light and fluffy. Beat in flour and vanilla; stir in coconut and walnuts. Mound 1 teaspoonful onto each cookie. Drizzle with chocolate; let stand until set.

YIELD: 3 DOZEN.

DIPPED LEMON SPRITZ

dipped lemon spritz

PREP 50 min.
BAKE 10 min. + cooling

LEE ROBERTS • RACINE, WISCONSIN

These dipped squares are sure to be a hit on your holiday cookie plate. The crisp treats please everyone's chocolate cravings.

2/3 cup plus 2 tablespoons sugar
2 teaspoons grated lemon peel
1 cup unsalted butter, softened
1 egg
2 teaspoons lemon juice
1 teaspoon vanilla extract
2-1/2 cups all-purpose flour
1/4 teaspoon baking powder
Dash salt
1 package (12 ounces) dark chocolate chips

- In a small food processor, combine sugar and lemon peel; cover and process until blended. In a large bowl, cream butter and 2/3 cup lemon-sugar until light and fluffy. Beat in the egg, lemon juice and vanilla. Combine the flour, baking powder and salt; gradually add to creamed mixture and mix well.

- Using a cookie press fitted with a 1-1/2-in. bar disk, form the dough into long strips on ungreased baking sheets. Cut each of the strips into squares (there is no need to separate the pieces).

- Bake at 350° for 8-10 minutes or until set (do not brown). Remove to wire racks to cool completely.

- In a microwave, melt chocolate; stir until smooth. Dip cookies diagonally in chocolate, allowing excess to drip off. Place on waxed paper; sprinkle chocolate with remaining lemon sugar. Let stand until set. Store in an airtight container at room temperature, or freeze for up to 3 months.

YIELD: 6 DOZEN.

coconut cream rounds

PREP 45 min.
BAKE 10 min. + cooling

SYLVIA THURSTON DAVIS • AUBURN, NEW YORK

With a yummy coconut topping, these goodies are a holiday hit, tea-party favorite and potluck-dinner "must." I've been using this recipe for more than 50 years.

chewy ginger cookies

PREP 15 min.
BAKE 10 min.

BERNICE SMITH • STURGEON LAKE, MINNESOTA

These moist, delicious ginger cookies have an old-fashioned appeal that'll take you back to Grandma's kitchen. I'm never surprised when these treats quickly disappear from my cookie jar.

3/4 cup shortening
1-1/4 cups sugar, *divided*
1 egg
1/4 cup molasses
1 teaspoon vanilla extract
2 cups all-purpose flour
1 teaspoon ground cinnamon
1 teaspoon ground ginger
1 teaspoon baking soda

1/2 teaspoon salt

1/2 teaspoon ground cloves

- In a large bowl, cream shortening and 1 cup sugar until light and fluffy. Beat in the egg, molasses and vanilla. Combine dry ingredients; add to creamed mixture and mix well.

- Roll into 1-in. balls; roll in remaining sugar. Place 1-1/2 in. apart on ungreased baking sheets.

- Bake at 375° for 10 minutes or until lightly browned. Remove to wire racks. Store in an airtight container.

YIELD: ABOUT 4 DOZEN.

macaroon kisses

PREP 45 min. + chilling

BAKE 10 min. + cooling

LEE ROBERTS • RACINE, WISCONSIN

These macaroon kisses are sure to delight lovers of coconut and chocolate. The sweet combination is simply irresistible.

1/3 cup butter, softened

1 package (3 ounces) cream cheese, softened

3/4 cup sugar

1 egg yolk

2 teaspoons almond extract

1-1/2 cups all-purpose flour

2 teaspoons baking powder

1/2 teaspoon salt

5 cups flaked coconut, *divided*

48 milk chocolate kisses

Coarse sugar

- In a large bowl, cream the butter, cream cheese and sugar until light and fluffy. Beat in egg yolk and extract. Combine the flour, baking powder and salt; gradually add to creamed mixture and mix well. Stir in 3 cups coconut. Cover and refrigerate for 1 hour or until dough is easy to handle.

- Roll into 1-in. balls and roll in the remaining coconut. Place 2 in. apart on ungreased baking sheets.

- Bake at 350° for 10-12 minutes or until lightly browned. Immediately press a chocolate kiss into the center of each cookie; sprinkle with coarse sugar. Cool on pan for 2-3 minutes or until chocolate is softened. Remove to wire racks to cool completely.

YIELD: 4 DOZEN.

MY KIDS' FAVORITE COOKIES

my kids' favorite cookies

PREP 15 min.

BAKE 10 min.

ARDYS SMITH • PALO ALTO, CALIFORNIA

When I made these cookies during my mommy years, it was a real challenge to keep my young sons out of the kitchen to let the snacks cool. I still enjoy making these mouthwatering morsels for my grown-up boys today.

1 cup butter, softened

1/2 cup sugar

1/2 cup packed brown sugar

1 egg

1 teaspoon vanilla extract

2 cups all-purpose flour

1 teaspoon baking soda

1/2 teaspoon salt

1-1/2 cups quick-cooking oats

1 cup flaked coconut

5 milk chocolate candy bars (1.55 ounces *each*)

- In a large bowl, cream butter and sugars until light and fluffy. Beat in egg and vanilla. Combine the flour, baking soda and salt; gradually add to creamed mixture and mix well. Beat in oats and coconut.

- Roll into 1-in. balls. Place cookies 2 in. apart on ungreased baking sheets; flatten slightly. Bake at 350° for 10-12 minutes or until lightly browned.

- Break each candy bar into 12 pieces; press a chocolate piece into the center of each warm cookie. Remove to wire racks.

YIELD: 5 DOZEN.

EDITOR'S NOTE: This recipe was tested with Hershey's premier baking pieces.

MACAROON KISSES

SURPRISE CRINKLES

surprise crinkles

PREP 25 min.

BAKE 15 min.

LOLA FENSKY • MOUNDRIDGE, KANSAS

I created this recipe by trial and error using many different kinds of candy. Milky Ways were the secret "surprise" my family liked best.

    1   cup shortening
  1/2   cup butter, softened
    2   cups packed brown sugar
    1   cup sugar
    3   eggs
1-1/2   teaspoons vanilla extract
4-1/4   cups all-purpose flour
1-1/2   teaspoons baking soda
  1/4   teaspoon ground cinnamon
  1/8   teaspoon salt
    2   packages (13.3 ounces *each*)
        fun-size Milky Way candy bar

• In a large bowl, cream the shortening, butter and sugars until light and fluffy. Add eggs, one at a time, beating well after each addition. Beat in vanilla. Combine the flour, baking soda, cinnamon and salt; gradually add to the creamed mixture and mix well.

• Roll the dough into 1-1/2-in. balls. Cut each candy bar into fourths; push one portion into the center of each ball, completely covering the candy with dough. Place 2 in. apart onto ungreased baking sheets.

• Bake at 350° for 12-14 minutes or until golden brown and surface cracks. Remove to wire racks to cool.

YIELD: 9 DOZEN.

butter crunch cookies

PREP 15 min.

BAKE 10 min.

MONIQUE SWALLOW • CORPUS CHRISTI, TEXAS

I've passed along this easy recipe to more people than any other one I have stuffed in my files. Cornflakes and pecans give these gems their delightful crunch.

    2   cups butter, softened
    2   cups sugar
    3   cups all-purpose flour
    2   teaspoons cream of tartar
    2   teaspoons baking soda
  1/2   teaspoon salt
    4   cups cornflakes, lightly crushed
    1   cup chopped pecans

• In a large bowl, cream butter and sugar until light and fluffy. Combine the flour, cream of tartar, baking soda and salt; gradually add to the creamed mixture and mix well. Stir in the cornflakes and pecans.

• Roll into 1-in. balls. Place 1 in. apart on ungreased baking sheets. Bake at 350° for 10-12 minutes or until lightly browned. Cool for 2 minutes before removing to wire racks.

YIELD: ABOUT 8 DOZEN.

oatmeal gingersnaps

PREP 20 min.

BAKE 10 min.

SHERRY HARKE • SOUTH BEND, INDIANA

I always get compliments on these delicious and chewy cookies. The spicy aroma fills my kitchen when they're baking and never fails to set a warm mood.

  1/2   cup shortening
    1   cup sugar
    1   egg
  1/4   cup molasses
1-1/2   cups all-purpose flour
  3/4   cup quick-cooking oats
    1   teaspoon baking soda
    1   teaspoon ground ginger
  1/4   teaspoon salt
  1/4   teaspoon ground cloves
Additional sugar

• In a large bowl, cream shortening and sugar until light and fluffy. Beat in egg and molasses. Combine the dry ingredients; gradually add to creamed mixture and mix well. Roll into 1-in. balls; roll in additional sugar.

• Place 2 in. apart on greased baking sheets. Flatten with a glass dipped in sugar. Bake at 350° for 10 minutes or until set (do not overbake). Remove to wire racks to cool.

YIELD: ABOUT 3-1/2 DOZEN.

chocolate-dipped coconut snowballs

PREP 20 min.

BAKE 10 min. + chilling

EMILY BARRETT • WYOMING, PENNSYLVANIA

If you like the taste of coconut and chocolate, you won't be able to help falling in love with these fun, change-of-pace snowballs.

  1/3   cup butter, softened
  2/3   cup packed brown sugar
    1   egg
  1/2   teaspoon vanilla extract
1-1/3   cups all-purpose flour
  1/4   teaspoon baking powder
  1/4   teaspoon baking soda
  1/4   teaspoon salt
    4   ounces German sweet chocolate, finely chopped
  1/2   cup flaked coconut
  1/2   cup finely chopped pecans, toasted
  TOPPING:
   12   ounces semisweet chocolate, chopped
    4   teaspoons shortening
2-1/2   cups flaked coconut, toasted

• In a large bowl, cream butter and brown sugar until light and fluffy. Beat in egg and vanilla. Combine the flour, baking powder, baking soda and salt; gradually add to creamed mixture and mix well. Stir in the German sweet chocolate, coconut and pecans.

• Roll into 3/4-in. balls. Place 2 in. apart on ungreased baking sheets. Bake at 350° for 10-12 minutes or until edges are browned. Remove to wire racks to cool.

• In a microwave, melt semisweet chocolate and shortening; stir until smooth. Dip tops of cookies into chocolate mixture; allow excess to drip off. Place on waxed paper-lined baking sheets; sprinkle with toasted coconut. Chill for 1 hour or until firm.

YIELD: ABOUT 5-1/2 DOZEN.

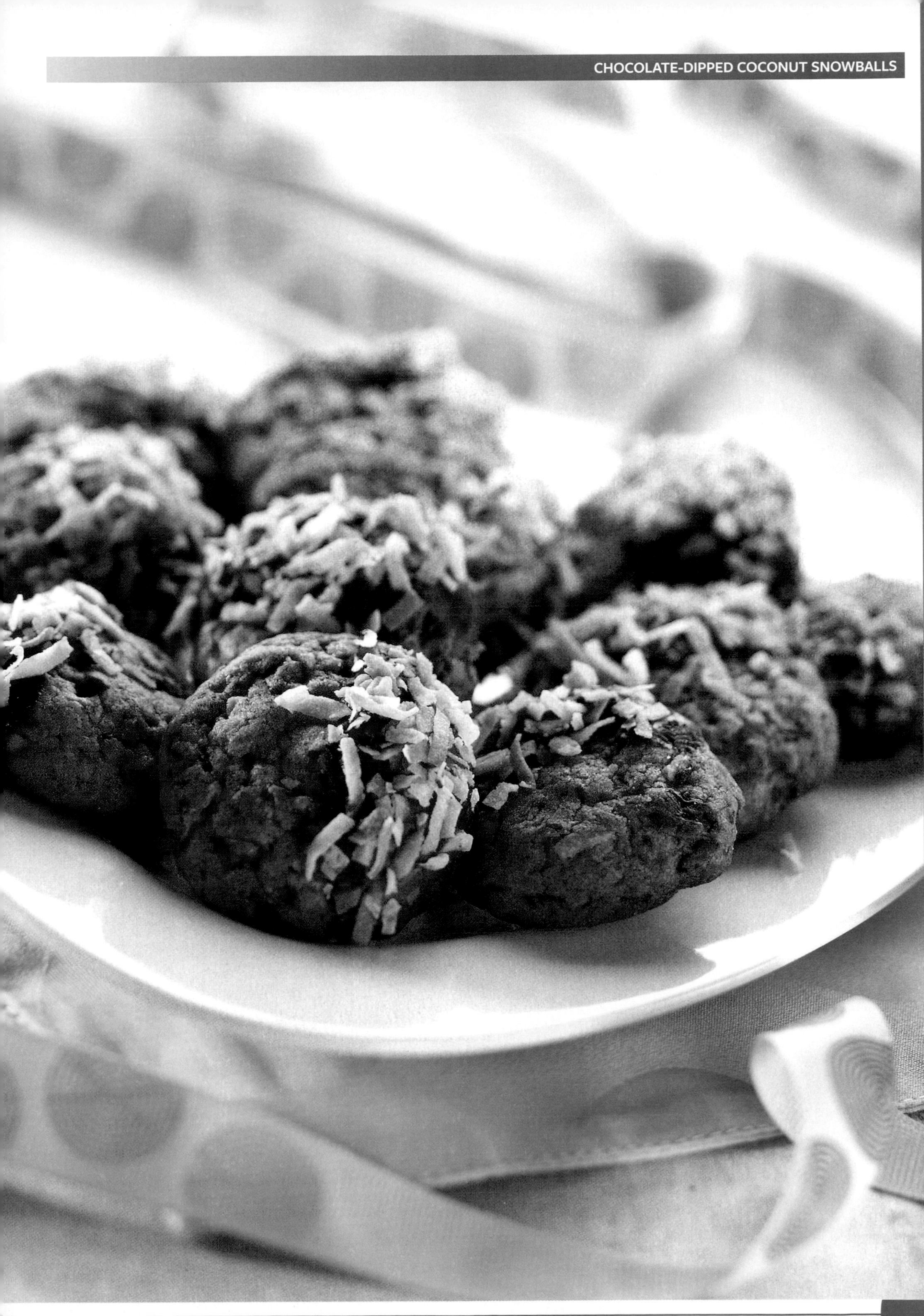

chocolate & vanilla spritz

PREP 40 min.
BAKE 10 min. + cooling

MARY BETH JUNG
HENDERSONVILLE, NORTH CAROLINA

These tender treats are so cute and have a nice buttery flavor. The dough is easy to work with and the cookies bake up beautiful and delicious every time.

- 1-1/2 cups butter, softened
- 1 cup sugar
- 1 egg
- 2 tablespoons 2% milk
- 1 teaspoon vanilla extract
- 1/2 teaspoon almond extract
- 3-1/2 cups all-purpose flour
- 1 teaspoon baking powder
- 3 tablespoons baking cocoa

Melted chocolate and chocolate jimmies, optional

- In a large bowl, cream the butter and sugar until light and fluffy. Beat in the egg, milk and extracts. Combine the flour and baking powder; gradually add dry ingredients to the creamed mixture and mix well.

- Divide dough in half; add cocoa to one portion and mix well. Divide each portion into six pieces; shape each into a 5-in. log. Place a chocolate log and vanilla log together, pressing to form another log.

- Using a cookie press fitted with the disk of your choice, press dough 2 in. apart onto ungreased baking sheets. Bake at 375° for 9-11 minutes or until edges are lightly browned. Remove to wire racks to cool.

- If desired, dip each cookie halfway into the melted chocolate, allowing excess to drip off. Place on waxed paper; sprinkle with jimmies. Let stand until set.

YIELD: 9 DOZEN.

java cream drops

PREP 35 min.
BAKE 10 min.

MARIA REGAKIS
SOMERVILLE, MASSACHUSETTS

My coworkers love coffee so whenever I come across a coffee-flavored recipe I'm sure to clip it for my files. These great-tasting treats are always a hit with my big group of java-loving friends!

CHOCOLATE & VANILLA SPRITZ

- 2 tablespoons instant coffee granules
- 1 tablespoon half-and-half cream
- 1 cup butter, softened
- 2/3 cup sugar
- 2/3 cup packed brown sugar
- 1 egg
- 1 teaspoon vanilla extract
- 2-1/4 cups all-purpose flour
- 1 teaspoon baking soda
- 1/4 teaspoon salt
- 1/4 cup baking cocoa
- 1/2 cup finely chopped walnuts
- 1/2 cup miniature semisweet chocolate chips

- In a small bowl, combine coffee granules and cream; set aside. In a large bowl, cream butter, sugar and brown sugar until light and fluffy. Beat in the egg, vanilla and reserved coffee mixture. Combine flour, baking soda and salt; gradually add to creamed mixture and mix well.

- Divide dough in half. To one portion, add cocoa and walnuts. Stir chocolate chips into remaining dough.

- To form cookies, place 1 teaspoon of each dough on an ungreased baking sheet; lightly press doughs together. Flatten slightly. Repeat with remaining doughs. Bake at 375° for 8-10 minutes. Cool for 1 minute before removing from pans to wire racks.

YIELD: 5 DOZEN.

chocolate pecan tassies

PREP 35 min. + chilling
BAKE 25 min. + cooling

LORAINE MEYER • BEND, OREGON

This recipe is part of our Christmas Eve buffet. These tassies have been called sinful by many friends and relatives and never last long.

- 1/2 cup butter, softened
- 1 package (3 ounces) cream cheese, softened
- 1 cup all-purpose flour

FILLING:

- 1 egg
- 1 tablespoon butter, melted and cooled
- 1 teaspoon vanilla extract
- 2/3 cup packed brown sugar

Dash salt

CRISP LEMON COOKIES

mocha nut balls

PREP 20 min.
BAKE 15 min.

JANET SULLIVAN • BUFFALO, NEW YORK

These tender, flavorful mocha balls are so addictive that I always know I have to make a double batch. My family demands it!

    1   cup butter, softened
    1/2 cup sugar
    2   teaspoons vanilla extract
1-3/4   cups all-purpose flour
    1/3 cup baking cocoa
    1   tablespoon instant coffee granules
    1   cup finely chopped pecans *or* walnuts
Confectioners' sugar

• In a large bowl, cream butter and sugar until light and fluffy. Beat in vanilla. Combine the flour, cocoa and coffee granules; gradually add to creamed mixture and mix well. Stir in pecans. Roll into 1-in. balls. Place 2 in. apart on ungreased baking sheets.

• Bake at 325° for 14-16 minutes or until firm. Cool on pans for 1-2 minutes before removing to wire racks. Roll warm cookies in confectioners' sugar.

YIELD: 4-1/2 DOZEN.

MOCHA NUT BALLS

    60 miniature milk chocolate kisses
    5   tablespoons chopped pecans

• In a small bowl, beat butter and cream cheese until smooth. Add flour; mix well. Cover and refrigerate for 1 hour or until easy to handle.

• In a small bowl, whisk the egg, butter, vanilla, brown sugar and salt until smooth; set aside. Shape dough into thirty 1-in. balls; press onto the bottom and up the sides of greased miniature muffin cups.

• Place a chocolate kiss in each cup. Fill each with 1 teaspoon brown sugar mixture; sprinkle with 1/2 teaspoon pecans.

• Bake at 325° for 24-26 minutes or until set. Lightly press a second chocolate kiss into the center of each cookie. Cool for 10 minutes before removing from pans to wire racks to cool completely. Store in an airtight container.

YIELD: 2-1/2 DOZEN.

 **tip**

flattened cookies

When a recipe instructs to flatten cookie dough with a sugar-dipped drinking glass, set the sugar aside and place parchment paper over the portions of dough on the baking sheet. The paper will prevent the dough from sticking to the glass and will easily lift away. Then sprinkle the sugar over the treats before popping them in the oven.

crisp lemon cookies

PREP 30 min.
BAKE 15 min. + cooling

DARLENE DIXON • HANOVER, MINNESOTA

You'll find these light citrus cookies are a nice change of pace from typical sugar cookies. Melted white baking chips drizzled over the top is a fantastic finishing touch.

1-1/3   cups butter, softened
    2   cups confectioners' sugar
    2   tablespoons lemon juice
    2   teaspoons grated lemon peel
    1/2 teaspoon vanilla extract
    3   cups all-purpose flour
    1/4 cup sugar
    3/4 cup white baking chips, melted

• In a large bowl, cream butter and confectioners' sugar until light and fluffy. Beat in the lemon juice, peel and vanilla. Gradually add flour and mix well.

• Shape dough into 1-in. balls. Place 2 in. apart on ungreased baking sheets. Coat the bottom of a glass with cooking spray; dip in sugar. Flatten cookies with glass, redipping in the sugar as needed.

• Bake at 325° for 11-13 minutes or until edges are lightly browned. Remove to wire racks to cool. Drizzle with melted chips.

YIELD: ABOUT 4-1/2 DOZEN.

chrusciki bow tie cookies

PREP 1 hour
COOK 5 min.

LINDA SVERCAUSKI • SAN DIEGO, CALIFORNIA

My late mother-in-law gave me the recipe for these traditional Polish "angel wings," and I like to make them in memory of her. My family is always excited to nibble on these sweet treats.

- 3 egg yolks
- 1 egg
- 1/4 cup spiced rum
- 2 tablespoons vanilla extract
- 1/2 teaspoon salt
- 1/4 cup confectioners' sugar
- 2 cups all-purpose flour

Oil for deep-fat frying
Additional confectioners' sugar

- In a large bowl, beat the egg yolks, egg, rum, vanilla and salt until blended. Gradually add confectioners' sugar; beat until smooth. Stir in flour until a stiff dough forms. Turn onto a lightly floured surface; knead seven times.

- Divide dough into three portions. Roll one portion into a 1/4-in.-thick rectangle, about 12 in. x 5-1/2 in. Cut in half lengthwise, then cut dough widthwise into 1-1/2-in.-wide strips. Cut a 3/4-in. lengthwise slit down the center of each strip; pull one of the ends through the slit, forming a bow. Repeat.

- In an electric skillet or deep-fat fryer, heat oil to 375°. Fry cookies, a few at a time, for 1-2 minutes on each side or until golden brown. Drain on paper towels. Dust with confectioners' sugar.

YIELD: 4 DOZEN.

calypso cups

PREP 30 min. + chilling
BAKE 15 min. + cooling

FRANK KACZMAREK • STEUBENVILLE, OHIO

These cups are great for all types of celebrations throughout the year. I simply tint the frosting for the occasion—red for Valentine's Day, blue or pink for baby showers and green for Christmas.

- 1 cup butter, softened
- 2 packages (3 ounces each) cream cheese, softened
- 2 cups all-purpose flour

CHRUSCIKI BOW TIE COOKIES

FILLING:

- 1/2 cup flaked coconut
- 1/2 cup sugar
- 1-1/2 teaspoons cornstarch
- 1 can (8 ounces) crushed pineapple, undrained
- 1 egg

FROSTING:

- 2 cups confectioners' sugar
- 1/2 cup shortening
- 1 teaspoon vanilla extract
- 3 to 4 tablespoons 2% milk

Finely chopped walnuts *and/or* additional flaked coconut, optional

- In a large bowl, beat butter and cream cheese until smooth. Gradually add flour and mix well. Cover and refrigerate for 1 hour or until easy to handle.

- Roll into 1-in. balls. Press onto the bottom and up the sides of greased miniature muffin cups. Combine the filling ingredients; spoon into cups.

- Bake at 350° for 15-20 minutes or until the edges are lightly browned. Cool in pans on wire racks.

- For frosting, combine the sugar, shortening and vanilla until smooth; add enough milk to achieve spreading consistency. Remove cooled cups from pans. Frost; sprinkle with walnuts and additional flaked coconut if desired.

YIELD: 4 DOZEN.

caramel tassies

PREP 1 hour
BAKE 15 min. + cooling

JANE BRICKER • SCOTTDALE, PENNSYLVANIA

These buttery tassies with a smooth caramel filling make a nice addition to a holiday dessert tray. These are one of my gang's favorites.

- 1 cup butter, softened
- 2 packages (3 ounces *each*) cream cheese, softened
- 2 cups all-purpose flour

FILLING:

- 1 package (14 ounces) caramels
- 1/4 cup plus 3 tablespoons evaporated milk

FROSTING:

- 2 tablespoons shortening
- 2 tablespoons butter, softened
- 1 cup confectioners' sugar
- 1 tablespoon evaporated milk

- In a large bowl, cream butter and cream cheese until light and fluffy. Gradually add flour and mix well. Cover and refrigerate for 1 hour or until easy to handle.

- Roll dough into 1-in. balls; press onto the bottom and up the sides of ungreased miniature muffin cups. Prick bottoms with a fork. Bake at 375° for 15-17 minutes or until golden brown. Cool for 5 minutes before removing from pans to wire racks.

- In a large heavy saucepan over low heat, melt caramels with milk. Remove from the heat; cool slightly. Transfer to a heavy-duty resealable plastic bag; cut a small hole in a corner of the bag. Pipe filling into pastry cups. Cool to room temperature.

- For frosting, in a small bowl, beat shortening and butter until smooth. Gradually beat in confectioners' sugar and milk until fluffy. Pipe onto filling. Store in the refrigerator.

YIELD: 4 DOZEN.

cream filberts

PREP 25 min.

BAKE 15 min. + cooling

DEANNA RICHTER ● ELMORE, MINNESOTA

These cookies remind me of the "mothball candy" I used to buy with dimes my grandmother gave me. The filbert, which is another name for a hazelnut, is a nice crunchy surprise in the middle.

    1   cup shortening
    3/4 cup sugar

    1   egg
    1   teaspoon vanilla extract
    2-1/2 cups all-purpose flour
    1/2 teaspoon baking powder
    1/8 teaspoon salt
    3/4 cup whole hazelnuts

GLAZE:

    2   cups confectioners' sugar
    3   tablespoons water
    2   teaspoons vanilla extract

Granulated sugar *or* about 60 crushed sugar cubes

- In a large bowl, cream shortening and sugar until light and fluffy. Beat in egg and vanilla. Combine the dry ingredients; gradually add to creamed mixture.

- Roll heaping teaspoonfuls of the dough into balls; press a hazelnut into each and reshape balls. Place cookies 2 in. apart on ungreased baking sheets.

- Bake cookies at 375° for 12-15 minutes or until lightly browned. Cool on wire racks. In a bowl, combine the confectioners' sugar, water and vanilla until smooth; dip the tops of cookies in glaze. Sprinkle with sugar.

YIELD: ABOUT 5 DOZEN.

CHOCOLATE CAKE COOKIES

chocolate cake cookies

PREP 30 min.

BAKE 10 min.

MONICA STOUT ● ANCHORAGE, ALASKA

I love these soft, chewy delights. They take just a few minutes to bake and are easy enough for kids to join in the fun of making them.

    1   package (18-1/4 ounces) chocolate fudge cake mix
    2   packages (3.9 ounces *each*) instant chocolate fudge pudding mix
    1-1/2 cups mayonnaise
    2   cups (12 ounces) semisweet chocolate chips
    1/2 cup chopped walnuts

- In a large bowl, combine cake mix, pudding mixes and mayonnaise; mix well. Stir in chocolate chips and walnuts.

- Shape by teaspoonfuls into balls; place on greased baking sheets. Bake at 350° for 9-10 minutes or until the cookies puff and surfaces cracks slightly. Cool for 5 minutes before removing from pans to wire racks.

YIELD: 7 DOZEN.

tip

shaping dough

To shape dough into a 1-in. ball, roll 2 teaspoons between your palms until it forms a ball. If the dough is sticky, you can refrigerate it until it is easy to handle, lightly flour your hands or lightly spray your hands with a little nonstick cooking spray.

CREAM FILBERTS

cutout cookies

Let your creativity loose by baking cutout cookies in all shapes and sizes to celebrate any holiday, season or special occasion.

SOUR CREAM SUGAR COOKIES

ginger leaf cutouts

PREP 1-1/4 hours + chilling
BAKE 10 min. + cooling

SUSAN FRANTZ • PITTSBURGH, PENNSYLVANIA

My father enjoyed these ginger delights with apple cider when he returned home from hunting on Thanksgiving morning.

    1   cup shortening
    1   cup sugar
    1   egg
    1   cup molasses
    2   tablespoons white vinegar
    5   cups all-purpose flour
2-1/2   teaspoons ground ginger
1-1/2   teaspoons baking soda
    1   teaspoon ground cinnamon
    1   teaspoon ground cloves
  1/2   teaspoon salt

- In a large bowl, cream shortening and sugar until light and fluffy. Beat in egg. Beat in molasses and vinegar. Combine the flour, ginger, baking soda, cinnamon, cloves and salt; gradually add to creamed mixture and mix well.

- Divide dough into fourths. Wrap each portion in plastic wrap; refrigerate for 4 hours or until easy to handle.

- On a lightly floured surface, roll out one portion of dough at a time to 1/8-in. thickness. Cut with floured 3-in. leaf-shaped cookie cutters. Place 1 in. apart on greased baking sheets. With a sharp knife, score veins in leaves.

- Bake at 375° for 6-8 minutes or until edges are firm and lightly browned. Remove to wire racks to cool. Store in an airtight container.

YIELD: 5 DOZEN.

GINGER LEAF CUTOUTS

sour cream sugar cookies

PREP 70 min. + chilling
BAKE 10 min. + cooling

CAROLYN WALTON • SMOOT, WYOMING

I make these cookies for my family and our neighbors every Valentine's Day. The heart-shaped treats stay soft for at least a week, and they look so pretty frosted bright pink and then piped with lacy frosting.

    1   cup shortening
    1   cup sugar
    1   egg
    1   cup (8 ounces) sour cream
1-1/2   teaspoons vanilla extract
    4   cups all-purpose flour
1-1/2   teaspoons baking soda
  1/4   teaspoon salt
FROSTING:
    1   cup butter, softened
    9   cups confectioners' sugar
    3   teaspoons vanilla extract
  2/3   to 3/4 cup 2% milk
        Paste food coloring

- In a large bowl, cream shortening and sugar until light and fluffy. Beat in the egg, sour cream and vanilla. Combine the flour, baking soda and salt; gradually add to creamed mixture and mix well. Cover and refrigerate for 1 hour or until easy to handle.

- On a lightly floured surface, roll dough to 1/4-in. thickness. Cut with a floured 3-in. heart-shaped cookie cutter.

- Place cookies 1 in. apart on baking sheets lightly coated with cooking spray. Bake at 350° for 8-10 minutes or until set. Allow to cool for 1 minute before removing to wire racks to cool completely.

- For frosting, in a large bowl, cream butter until light and fluffy. Beat in the confectioners' sugar and vanilla. Add enough milk to achieve desired consistency. Tint with food coloring. Decorate cookies as desired.

YIELD: ABOUT 4-1/2 DOZEN.

EDITOR'S NOTE: To create the look in the photo, use #10 and #4 round pastry tips.

CLASSIC SUGAR COOKIES

classic sugar cookies

PREP 2 hours + chilling
BAKE 10 min. + cooling

KRIISTINE FOSSMEYER • HUNTLEY, ILLINOIS

Take these scrumptious sugar cookies to a school party or a bake sale, and they will be the star of the show!

- 1-1/4 cups butter, softened
- 1-3/4 cups confectioners' sugar
- 2 ounces almond paste
- 1 egg
- 1/4 cup 2% milk
- 1 teaspoon vanilla extract
- 4 cups all-purpose flour
- 1/2 teaspoon salt

Wooden skewers *or* lollipop sticks

ICING:
- 2 cups confectioners' sugar
- 2-1/2 tablespoons evaporated milk

Food coloring of your choice

- In a large bowl, cream butter and confectioners' sugar until light and fluffy; add almond paste. Beat in the egg, milk and vanilla. Combine flour and salt; gradually add to creamed mixture and mix well. Cover and refrigerate for 1 hour.

- On a lightly floured surface, roll out dough to 1/4-in. thickness. Cut out with floured 3-in. cookie cutters. Place 1 in. apart on ungreased baking sheets. Insert skewers or sticks. Bake at 375° for 7-8 minutes or until firm. Let stand for 2 minutes before removing to wire racks to cool.

- In a large bowl, whisk confectioners' sugar and milk. Gently spread icing over cooled cookies; allow to dry completely. Tint the remaining icing with food coloring. Decorate as desired; allow icing to dry.

YIELD: ABOUT 2-1/2 DOZEN.

decorated easter cookies

PREP 30 min. + chilling
BAKE 10 min. + cooling

SUE GRONHOLZ • BEAVER DAM, WISCONSIN

Rich, buttery sensations like these never last long at a party. I use egg-shaped cutters and serve them as part of Easter brunch.

- 1 cup butter, softened
- 1 cup sugar
- 2 eggs
- 1/4 cup cold water
- 1 teaspoon vanilla extract

- 3-1/4 cups all-purpose flour
- 1 teaspoon baking soda
- 1/2 teaspoon salt

GLAZE:
- 2 cups confectioners' sugar
- 1/4 cup water
- 2 tablespoons light corn syrup

Food coloring

Decorator's gel

- In a bowl, cream butter and sugar. Add eggs, water and vanilla. Combine flour, baking soda and salt; gradually add to creamed mixture. Cover and chill for several hours.

- Roll out dough on a lightly floured surface to 1/4-in. thickness. Cut with an egg-shaped cookie cutter (or cutters with other Easter themes such as chicks or bunnies). Make a hole with a straw or toothpick in the top of at least 27 cookies.

- Place on greased baking sheets. Bake at 350° for 8-10 minutes or until light golden brown. Remove to wire racks; cool completely.

- For glaze, combine sugar, water and corn syrup until smooth. Depending on how many colors are desired, divide glaze into several small bowls and tint with food coloring. Using a small brush and stirring glaze often, brush glaze on cookies (or leave some plain if desired). Allow glazed cookies to harden for at least 1 hour.

- Add designs with tinted glaze or decorator's gel, referring to photo for ideas. Allow to dry.

YIELD: 7-8 DOZEN 2-1/2-IN. COOKIES.

tip

cutout cookies

Follow these easy tips for successful cutout cookies. For easier handling, chill the dough for 1 to 2 hours before rolling it out. Lightly flour the surface and rolling pin. Roll out the dough as evenly as possible to the recommended thickness. Dip the cookie cutter in flour, then press the cutter into the dough. Lift each cookie with a small metal spatula to support the cookie as it is moved to the baking sheet. Bake according to recipe directions. With a metal spatula or pancake turner, remove cookies from the baking sheet to a wire rack, being careful to support the entire cookie. Cool completely before frosting or storing.

tea cookies

PREP 20 min. + chilling
BAKE 10 min. + cooling

CAROLYN KLINGENSMITH ● LIVONIA, MICHIGAN

My cookies are so simple, but have the look and taste of something you spent hours making.

- 2 cups butter, softened
- 1 cup sugar
- 1/4 cup sweetened condensed milk
- 1 teaspoon vanilla extract
- 4 cups all-purpose flour
- 1/8 teaspoon salt
- 1/3 cup ground almonds
- 1/4 cup seedless raspberry jam
- Confectioners' sugar

● In a large bowl, cream butter and sugar until light and fluffy. Beat in milk and vanilla. Combine flour and salt; gradually add to creamed mixture and mix well. Divide dough into five 1-cup portions; shape each into a 10-in.-long roll. Wrap individually in plastic wrap. Refrigerate for 1 hour or until easy to handle.

● On a lightly floured surface, roll dough to 1/8-in. thickness. Cut with a floured 2-1/2-in. round cookie cutter. Cut out the centers of half of the cookies with a 1-in. round cookie cutter (discard centers).

● Place 2 in. apart on ungreased baking sheets. Bake at 350° for 6-8 minutes or until edges are lightly browned. Cool for 2 minutes before removing to wire racks to cool completely.

● Spread each whole cookie with 1 teaspoon of jam; top with remaining cookies. Sprinkle with confectioners' sugar.

YIELD: 10 SANDWICH COOKIES.

shamrock cookies

PREP 25 min. + chilling
BAKE 10 min. + cooling

EDNA HOFFMAN ● HEBRON, INDIANA

These Irish sweets are yummy with a hint of mint flavor.

- 1 cup shortening
- 1 cup confectioners' sugar
- 1 egg
- 1 teaspoon peppermint extract
- 2-1/2 cups all-purpose flour
- 1 teaspoon salt
- Green paste food coloring
- Green colored sugar, optional

● In a large bowl, cream the shortening and confectioners' sugar until light and fluffy. Beat in egg and extract. Gradually add flour and salt. Tint with food coloring. Cover and refrigerate for 1 hour or until easy to handle.

● On a lightly floured surface, roll out dough to 1/4-in. thickness. Cut with a lightly floured 2-in. shamrock cookie cutter. Place 1 in. apart on ungreased baking sheets. Sprinkle with colored sugar if desired.

ICE CREAM KOLACHKES

● Bake at 375° for 10-12 minutes or until edges are lightly browned. Cool for 1 minute before removing to wire racks.

YIELD: 3 DOZEN.

ice cream kolachkes

PREP 1 hour + chilling
BAKE 10 min.

DIANE TURNER ● BRUNSWICK, OHIO

These traditional pastries are often filled with poppy seeds, nuts, jam or a mashed fruit mixture.

- 2 cups butter, softened
- 1 pint vanilla ice cream, softened
- 4 cups all-purpose flour
- 2 tablespoons sugar
- 2 cans (12 ounces *each*) apricot *and/or* raspberry cake and pastry filling
- 1 to 2 tablespoons confectioners' sugar, optional

● In the bowl of a heavy-duty stand mixer, beat butter and ice cream until blended (mixture will appear curdled). Add flour and sugar; mix well. Divide into four portions; cover and refrigerate for 2 hours or until easy to handle.

● On a lightly floured surface, roll one portion of dough into a 12-in. x 10-in. rectangle; cut into 2-in. squares. Place a teaspoonful of filling in the center of each square. Overlap two opposite corners of dough over filling; pinch tightly to seal. Place 2 in. apart on ungreased baking sheets. Repeat with remaining dough and filling.

● Bake at 350° for 11-14 minutes or until bottoms are lightly browned. Cool for 1 minute before removing from pans to wire racks. Sprinkle with confectioners' sugar if desired.

YIELD: 10 DOZEN.

TEA COOKIES

cream cheese cutouts

PREP 15 min. + chilling
BAKE 10 min. + cooling

JULIE DAWSON • GALENA, OHIO

Decorating goodies puts me in a happy mood. Cookies baked from this recipe won't rise too much in the oven or lose their shape.

- 1 cup butter, softened
- 1 package (3 ounces) cream cheese, softened
- 1 cup sugar
- 1 egg
- 1 teaspoon vanilla extract
- 2-1/2 cups all-purpose flour
- 1/4 teaspoon salt

FROSTING:

- 3 cups confectioners' sugar
- 1/3 cup butter, softened
- 1-1/2 teaspoons vanilla extract
- 2 to 3 tablespoons 2% milk

Food coloring, optional
Assorted sprinkles, optional

- In a large bowl, cream the butter, cream cheese and sugar until light and fluffy. Beat in egg and vanilla. Combine flour and salt; gradually add to creamed mixture just until blended. Cover and refrigerate for 1-2 hours or until easy to handle.

- On a lightly floured surface, roll the dough to 1/8-in. thickness. Cut with cookie cutters dipped in flour. Place 1 in. apart on ungreased baking sheets. Bake at 375° for 7-8 minutes or until edges are lightly browned. Cool for 1 minute before removing to wire racks.

CREAM CHEESE CUTOUTS

SUGAR STAR & FLAG COOKIES

- In a small bowl, beat the confectioners' sugar, butter, vanilla and enough milk to achieve desired consistency. Add food coloring if desired. Decorate cookies with frosting and sprinkles if desired.

YIELD: ABOUT 7 DOZEN.

sugar star & flag cookies

PREP 1-1/4 hours + chilling
BAKE 10 min. + cooling

SUSAN WHETZEL • PEARISBURG, VIRGINIA

A favorite treat to send to troops overseas, these soft sugar cutouts ship well and taste great!

- 1 cup butter, softened
- 1/2 cup cream cheese, softened
- 2 cups sugar
- 4 eggs
- 1-1/2 teaspoons vanilla extract
- 1 teaspoon lemon extract
- 5 cups all-purpose flour
- 2 teaspoons baking powder
- 1 teaspoon salt

Decorating icing *and/or* colored sugars

- In a large bowl, cream the butter, cream cheese and sugar until light and fluffy. Beat in eggs and extracts. Combine the flour, baking powder and salt; gradually add to creamed mixture and mix well. Cover and refrigerate for 2 hours or until easy to handle.

- On a lightly floured surface, roll out dough to 1/4-in. thickness. Cut with floured 2- to 3-in. cookie cutters. Place 1 in. apart on ungreased baking sheets. Sprinkle with colored sugars as desired.

- Bake at 350° for 9-11 minutes or until set. Cool for 2 minutes before removing from pans to wire racks to cool completely. Decorate with icing and additional sugars if desired.

YIELD: 10 DOZEN.

maple sugar cookies

PREP 15 min. + chilling
BAKE 10 min.

ANNA GLAUS • GREENSBURG, PENNSYLVANIA

This recipe is requested by friends and family every time I'm asked to bring something for an event. Folks enjoy the subtle maple flavor in this crisp delight.

- 1 cup butter-flavored shortening
- 1-1/4 cups sugar
- 2 eggs

1/4 cup maple syrup

3 teaspoons vanilla extract

3 cups all-purpose flour

3/4 teaspoon baking powder

1/2 teaspoon baking soda

1/2 teaspoon salt

- In a large bowl, cream shortening and sugar until light and fluffy. Add eggs, one at a time, beating well after each addition. Beat in syrup and vanilla. Combine the remaining ingredients; gradually add to the creamed mixture and mix well. Cover and refrigerate for 2 hours or until easy to handle.

- On a lightly floured surface, roll out dough to 1/8-in. thickness. Cut with a floured 2-1/2-in. cookie cutter. Place 1 in. apart on ungreased baking sheets.

- Bake at 350° for 9-12 minutes or until golden brown. Remove to wire racks to cool.

YIELD: 4 DOZEN.

island swim dessert

PREP 1 hour + standing

BAKE 45 min. + cooling

SARA MARTIN ● BROOKFIELD, WISCONSIN

This awesome summer snack is not only fun to make but it's delicious, too. I had a great time making this with my mom. Decorate the cookies to look like your swimming suit or the colors of your party.

CREAM PUFF LAYER:

1 cup water

1/2 cup butter, cubed

1 cup all-purpose flour

4 eggs

COOKIES:

1 tube (16-1/2 ounces) refrigerated sugar cookie dough

2 cups confectioners' sugar

1/4 cup water

2 tablespoons light corn syrup

Food coloring

Red, blue and yellow writing icing

Assorted jumbo nonpareils

FILLING:

1 package (8 ounces) cream cheese, softened

3-1/2 cups cold milk

2 packages (3.9 ounces *each*) instant chocolate pudding mix

1 carton (8 ounces) frozen whipped topping, thawed

Blue food coloring

ISLAND:

3 Pirouette cookies

Granulated sugar

Spearmint leaf candies

2 tablespoons graham cracker crumbs

- In a large saucepan, bring water and butter to a boil over medium heat. Add flour all at once; stir until a smooth ball forms. Remove from the heat; let stand for 5 minutes. Add eggs, one at a time, beating well after each addition. Continue beating until mixture is smooth and shiny.

- Spread mixture into a greased 3-qt. baking dish. Bake at 400° for 30-35 minutes or until puffed and golden brown. Cool completely on a wire rack. Reduce heat to 350°.

- Roll out cookie dough to 1/4-in. thickness. With floured 3-in. and 4-1/4-in. gingerbread boy cookie cutters, cut out 12 swimmers. Re-roll scraps; cut out 1-1/2-in. circles for beach balls. Place on ungreased baking sheets. Bake at 350° for 11-13 minutes or until the edges are lightly browned. Remove to wire racks to cool completely.

- For the glaze, combine the confectioners' sugar, water and corn syrup until smooth. Divide glaze among small bowls; tint with the food coloring as desired. Using a small brush and stirring the glaze often, brush glaze over cookies. Allow glazed cookies to set for at least 1 hour. Add designs with the writing icing and nonpareils as desired.

- For filling, in a large bowl, beat the cream cheese, milk and pudding mixes until smooth. Spread over the puff layer; refrigerate for 20 minutes. Set aside 2 tablespoons of whipped topping for crests of waves; stir blue food coloring into remaining topping. Spread over filling; swirl, forming waves. Form crests with reserved topping. Cover and refrigerate until chilled.

- Meanwhile, for palm trees, break or cut 1 in. from one Pirouette cookie and 1-1/2 in. from another Pirouette. Leave remaining Pirouette full length.

- Sprinkle sugar on a work surface. For each palm tree, place three spearmint leaves on sugared surface. With a rolling pin, roll out each into an oval; cut out into a palm leaf shape. Using spearmint leaf scraps, attach three palm leaves to each Pirouette cookie; place flat. Let stand, uncovered, until set.

- Just before serving, sprinkle the corner of the dessert with cracker crumbs for an island; position the trees in sand. Add swimmers and a beach ball to the water. Serve dessert with additional cookies.

YIELD: 1 CENTERPIECE AND 18 COOKIES.

ISLAND SWIM DESSERT

sugar doves

PREP 30 min. + chilling
BAKE 10 min.

PEGGY PRESTON • FENTON, IOWA

These pretty little sugar doves are great for any occasion celebrating peace, love or hope. I enjoy spending a winter evening baking and decorating these beautiful cookies.

- 1 cup butter, softened
- 2 cups sugar
- 2 eggs
- 2 tablespoons milk
- 2 teaspoons vanilla extract
- 4-1/4 cups all-purpose flour
- 2 teaspoons baking powder
- 1/4 teaspoon salt

FROSTING:

- 1/2 cup shortening
- 3-3/4 cups confectioners' sugar
- 2 tablespoons milk
- 1 teaspoon almond extract
- 1/2 teaspoon vanilla extract
- 1 to 2 tablespoons water
- 4-1/2 cups sliced almonds
- 3-1/2 cups finely chopped walnuts

Miniature semisweet chocolate chips

- In a large bowl, cream butter and sugar until light and fluffy. Add eggs, one at a time, beating well after each addition. Beat in the milk and vanilla.

- Combine the flour, baking powder and salt; gradually add to creamed mixture and mix

well. Refrigerate dough for 2 hours or until easy to handle.

- On a lightly floured surface, roll out dough to 1/8-in. thickness. Cut with a 3-in. bird-shaped cookie cutter. Place 1 in. apart on greased baking sheets. Bake at 350° for 7-9 minutes or until set. Remove to wire racks to cool.

- For the frosting, in a small bowl, combine the shortening, confectioners' sugar, milk, extracts and enough water to achieve spreading consistency.

- Frost cookies. Arrange the almonds over the bodies and walnuts over the heads. Add chocolate chip eyes.

YIELD: 7-1/2 DOZEN.

chocolate walnut crescents

PREP 40 min. + chilling
BAKE 10 min. + cooling

TERRYANN MOORE • VINELAND, NEW JERSEY

I use a round cookie cutter to form the crescent shapes for these nutty favorites. They look so tantalizing sprinkled with sugar and drizzled with melted chocolate.

- 1 cup butter, softened
- 1/2 cup sugar
- 1 teaspoon vanilla extract
- 2 cups all-purpose flour
- 2 cups ground walnuts
- 3 tablespoons baking cocoa
- 2 to 3 tablespoons confectioners' sugar
- 1 package (12 ounces) semisweet chocolate chips
- 2 teaspoons shortening

- In a large bowl, cream butter and sugar until light and fluffy. Beat in vanilla. Combine the flour, walnuts and cocoa; gradually add to creamed mixture and mix well. Cover and refrigerate for 1 hour or until easy to handle.

- On a lightly floured surface, roll out dough to 1/4-in. thickness. Using a floured, plain or finely scalloped 2-in. round cookie cutter, cut a semicircle off one corner of the dough, forming the inside of a crescent shape. Reposition cutter 1-1/4 in. from inside of crescent; cut cookie, forming a crescent 1-1/4 in. wide at its widest point. Repeat. Chill and reroll scraps if desired.

- Place 1 in. apart on ungreased baking sheets. Bake at 350° for 9-11 minutes or until set. Cool for 1 minute before removing to wire racks to cool completely.

- Sprinkle cookies with confectioners' sugar. In a microwave, melt the chocolate chips and shortening; stir until smooth. Drizzle over the cookies; let stand until set. Store cookies in an airtight container.

YIELD: 10-1/2 DOZEN.

lemon stars

PREP 35 min. + chilling
BAKE 10 min. + cooling

JACQUELINE HILL • NORWALK, OHIO

Each one of these cookies has a citrus zing and a light, crunchy texture. The star shape makes them ideal for any celebration.

- 1/2 cup butter-flavored shortening
- 1 cup sugar
- 1 egg
- 1-1/2 teaspoons lemon extract
- 1/2 cup sour cream
- 1 teaspoon grated lemon peel
- 2-3/4 cups all-purpose flour
- 1/2 teaspoon baking soda
- 1/2 teaspoon salt

FROSTING:

- 1-1/2 cups confectioners' sugar
- 6 tablespoons butter
- 3/4 teaspoon lemon extract
- 3 drops yellow food coloring, optional
- 3 to 4 tablespoons 2% milk

Yellow colored sugar, optional

- In a large bowl, cream shortening and sugar until light and fluffy. Beat in egg and extract. Stir in sour cream and peel. Combine the flour, baking soda and salt; gradually add to creamed mixture and mix well. Divide dough into three balls; cover and refrigerate for 3 hours or until easy to handle.

- Remove one portion of dough from the refrigerator at a time. On a lightly floured surface, roll out dough to 1/4-in. thickness. Cut with a floured 2-in. star cookie cutter. Place 1 in. apart on ungreased baking sheets.

- Bake at 375° for 6-8 minutes or until edges are lightly browned. Remove cookies to wire racks to cool.

- For frosting, in a small bowl, combine the confectioners' sugar, butter, extract, food coloring if desired and enough milk to achieve spreading consistency. Frost cookies; sprinkle with colored sugar if desired.

YIELD: 9 DOZEN.

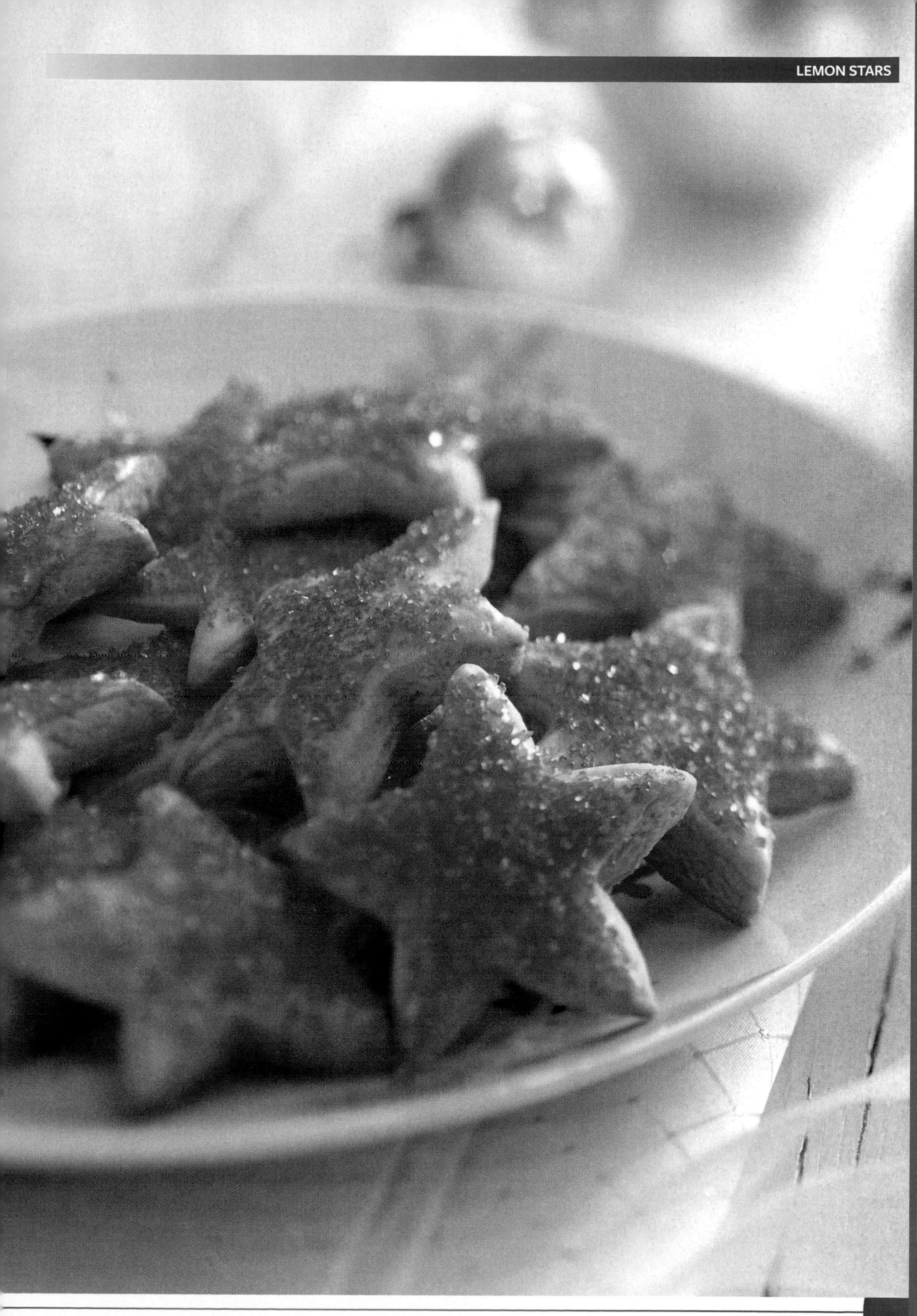

WALNUT CHOCOLATE HEARTS

walnut chocolate hearts

PREP 30 min. + chilling
BAKE 10 min. + cooling

MARIA HULL • BARTLETT, ILLINOIS

I've been making these cute hearts with Mom since I was a little girl. The recipe is one of my favorites and so quick to make.

- 1 cup butter, cubed
- 2/3 cup packed brown sugar
- 1 teaspoon vanilla extract
- 1 egg, lightly beaten
- 2-1/4 cups all-purpose flour
- 1/4 cup baking cocoa
- 1/2 teaspoon salt
- 3/4 cup finely chopped walnuts

TOPPING:

- 1-1/2 cups semisweet chocolate chips
- 2 tablespoons shortening
- 1/2 cup ground walnuts

● In a large saucepan, combine butter and brown sugar. Cook and stir over medium-low heat until butter is melted. Remove from the heat; stir in vanilla. Cool for 15 minutes. Stir in egg.

● Combine the flour, cocoa and salt; add to butter mixture. Fold in walnuts. Cover and chill for 30 minutes or until easy to handle.

● On a lightly floured surface, roll dough to 1/4-in. thickness. Cut with a floured 3-in. heart-shaped cookie cutter. Place 1 in. apart on ungreased baking sheets.

● Bake at 350° for 9-10 minutes or until edges are firm. Remove to wire racks to cool.

● For topping, in a microwave, melt chocolate chips and shortening; stir until smooth. Dip half of each heart into chocolate mixture; allow excess to drip off. Dip edges of dipped side into ground walnuts. Place on waxed paper; let stand until set.

YIELD: ABOUT 4 DOZEN.

frosted molasses cookies

PREP 40 min. + chilling
BAKE 10 min. + standing

SARAH BYLER • HARRISVILLE, PENNSYLVANIA

My family will come running the moment they smell these molasses sensations baking in the oven.

- 1 cup butter, softened
- 1 cup sugar

- 3 egg yolks
- 1 cup molasses
- 1/2 cup water
- 5 cups all-purpose flour
- 3 teaspoons baking soda
- 1-1/2 teaspoons ground cinnamon
- 1 teaspoon baking powder

FROSTING:

- 1-1/2 cups sugar
- 3 egg whites
- 1/4 cup water
- 1 cup confectioners' sugar

● In a large bowl, cream butter and sugar until light and fluffy. Beat in the egg yolks, molasses and water. Combine flour, baking soda, cinnamon and baking powder; gradually add to creamed mixture and mix well. Cover and refrigerate for 2 hours or until easy to handle.

● On a lightly floured surface, roll out dough to 1/8-in. thickness. Cut with a floured 2-1/2-in. round cookie cutter. Place 1 in. apart on ungreased baking sheets. Bake at 375° for 8-10 minutes or until edges are firm. Remove to wire racks to cool.

● For frosting, combine sugar, egg whites and water in a small heavy saucepan over low heat. With a hand mixer, beat on low speed for 1 minute. Continue beating on low over low heat until frosting reaches 160°, about 8-10 minutes. Pour into the bowl of a heavy-duty stand mixer; add confectioners' sugar. Beat on high until frosting forms stiff peaks, about 7 minutes. Frost cookies. Let stand until dry.

YIELD: 8 DOZEN.

berry-topped stars

PREP 45 min.
BAKE 10 min. + cooling

TASTE OF HOME TEST KITCHEN

Our Test Kitchen created this recipe that starts with convenient store-bought cookie dough. The treats are sure to be the star of your Fourth of July celebrations.

- 1 tube (18 ounces) refrigerated sugar cookie dough, softened
- 1/4 cup all-purpose flour
- 1 package (8 ounces) cream cheese, softened
- 1/3 cup confectioners' sugar
- 24 small fresh strawberries, thinly sliced
- 4 large kiwifruit, peeled and sliced or 1 cup fresh blueberries

- In a small bowl, combine cookie dough and flour until combined. Roll on a lightly floured surface to 1/4-in. thickness. Cut with a floured 3-in. star-shaped cookie cutter.

- Place 1 in. apart on ungreased baking sheets. Bake at 350° for 8-10 minutes or until edges are golden brown. Cool for 1 minute before removing to wire racks to cool completely.

- For frosting, in a small bowl, beat the cream cheese and confectioners' sugar until smooth. Set aside 1-2 tablespoons. Spread remaining frosting over cookies. Place five strawberry slices on each cookie. Using reserved frosting, attach one kiwi slice or 4-5 blueberries to each. Store in the refrigerator.

YIELD: 2 DOZEN.

strawberry valentine cookies

PREP 50 min.

BAKE 10 min. + cooling

MARNA HEITZ • FARLEY, IOWA

Start a new Valentine's Day tradition with these pretty, whimsical delights. The sweet strawberry flavor is a perfect complement to the chocolate glaze.

- 2/3 cup butter, softened
- 2/3 cup sugar
- 1 egg
- 1 tablespoon lemon juice
- 2 cups all-purpose flour
- 1/3 cup strawberry drink mix
- 2 teaspoons baking powder
- 1/2 teaspoon salt

GLAZE:
- 1 cup (6 ounces) semisweet chocolate chips
- 1 teaspoon shortening

FROSTING:
- 1/3 cup butter, softened
- 2 tablespoons strawberry drink mix
- 1/8 teaspoon salt
- 3 cups confectioners' sugar
- 3 to 5 tablespoons 2% milk

- In a small bowl, cream butter and sugar until light and fluffy. Beat in egg and lemon juice. Combine the flour, drink mix, baking powder and salt; gradually add to creamed mixture and mix well.

- On a lightly floured surface, roll out dough to 1/4-in. thickness. Cut dough with a floured 2-1/2- to 3-in. heart-shaped cookie cutter. Place 2 in. apart on ungreased baking sheets. Bake at 350° for 8-10 minutes or until set and edges begin to brown. Cool for 2 minutes before removing to wire racks to cool completely.

- In a microwave, melt chocolate chips and shortening; stir until smooth. Spread over the cookies; let stand until set.

- In a small bowl, beat the butter, drink mix and salt until blended. Gradually beat in confectioners' sugar. Add enough milk to achieve desired consistency. Decorate cookies.

YIELD: ABOUT 2 DOZEN.

CHOCOLATE SKELETON COOKIES

chocolate skeleton cookies

PREP 45 min.

BAKE 10 min. + cooling

LISA RUPPLE • KEENESBURG, COLORADO

Set out these cute treats for your next ghost and goblin party and watch them disappear!

- 1 cup butter, softened
- 1 cup sugar
- 1/2 cup packed brown sugar
- 1 egg
- 1 teaspoon vanilla extract
- 2-3/4 cups all-purpose flour
- 1/2 cup baking cocoa
- 1 teaspoon baking soda
- 1-1/2 cups confectioners' sugar
- 2 tablespoons 2% milk

- In a large bowl, cream the butter and sugars until light and fluffy. Beat in the egg and vanilla. Combine the flour, cocoa and baking soda; gradually add to the creamed mixture and mix well. Cover and refrigerate for 1-2 hours or until easy to handle.

- On a lightly floured surface, roll dough to 1/8-in. thickness. Cut with a floured 3-in. gingerbread boy cookie cutter. Place on greased baking sheets.

- Bake at 375° for 7-8 minutes or until set. Cool for 1 minute before removing from pans to wire racks to cool completely.

- For the icing, in a small bowl, combine the confectioners' sugar and milk until smooth. Cut a small hole in the corner of a resealable plastic bag; fill with icing. Pipe skeleton bones on the cookies.

YIELD: 3 DOZEN.

STRAWBERRY VALENTINE COOKIES

cinnamon stars

PREP 15 min. + chilling
BAKE 15 min.

JEAN JONES • PEACHTREE CITY, GEORGIA

These gems will fill your home with an irresistible aroma as they bake. My grandmother made them every Christmas when I was a child. I have fond memories of helping her in the kitchen.

    1 cup butter, softened
    2 cups sugar
    2 eggs
2-3/4 cups all-purpose flour
  1/3 cup ground cinnamon

- In a large bowl, cream butter and sugar until light and fluffy. Add eggs, one at a time, beating well after each addition. Combine flour and cinnamon; gradually add to creamed mixture and mix well. Cover and refrigerate for 1 hour or until easy to handle.

- On a lightly floured surface, roll out to 1/4-in. thickness. Cut with a 2-1/2-in. star-shaped cookie cutter dipped in flour. Place 1 in. apart on ungreased baking sheets.

- Bake at 350° for 15-18 minutes or until edges are firm and bottom of cookies are lightly browned. Remove to wire racks to cool.

YIELD: 5 DOZEN.

PINWHEEL COOKIES

CINNAMON STARS

pinwheel cookies

PREP 20 min. + chilling
BAKE 10 min.

HELEN BURCH • JAMESTOWN, NEW YORK

These colorful treats are as pretty to look at as they are to eat! Kids go crazy for their pinwheel shape.

    1 cup butter, softened
    1 cup confectioners' sugar
    1 egg
1-1/2 teaspoons almond extract
    1 teaspoon vanilla extract
2-1/2 cups all-purpose flour
    1 teaspoon salt
Red colored sugar
Red and green candied cherries, quartered

- In a large bowl, cream butter and confectioners' sugar until light and fluffy. Add egg and extracts; mix well. Combine flour and salt; gradually add to creamed mixture. Divide dough in half; wrap in plastic wrap. Chill overnight or until firm.

- On a lightly floured surface, roll out one portion of dough into a 12-in. x 10-in. rectangle, about 1/8 in. thick. Cut into 2-in. squares. In each square, make 1-in. slits in each corner. Bring every other corner up into center to form a pinwheel; press lightly. Sprinkle cookies with red sugar and press a candied cherry piece into the center of each.

- Place 1 in. apart on ungreased baking sheets. Bake at 350° for 8-10 minutes. Cool 1-2 minutes before removing to wire racks.

YIELD: ABOUT 4 DOZEN.

welsh tea cakes

PREP 15 min.
BAKE 15 min.

WENDY LEHMAN • HURON, OHIO

My old-fashioned cookies are crisp on the outside and slightly chewy on the inside, which is full of currants. I like to sprinkle the tops with sugar to enhance their sweetness and give them a lovely appearance.

2-1/2 cups all-purpose flour
    1 cup cold butter, cubed
  3/4 cup sugar
  1/4 cup quick-cooking oats
  1/2 teaspoon ground nutmeg
    2 eggs
  1/4 cup 2% milk
    1 cup dried currants
Additional sugar, optional

- Place flour in a large bowl; cut in butter until mixture resembles coarse crumbs. Add the sugar, oats and nutmeg. Stir in the eggs and milk. Fold in currants.

- On a heavily floured surface, roll out dough to 1/4-in. thickness. Cut with a floured 2-1/2-in. round cookie cutter. Place cookies 2 in. apart on greased baking sheets. Sprinkle with sugar if desired.

- Bake at 350° for 12-16 minutes or until lightly browned. Remove to wire racks to cool.

YIELD: 3 DOZEN.

lucky leprechaun cookies

PREP 30 min. + chilling
BAKE 10 min. + cooling

TASTE OF HOME TEST KITCHEN

My yummy bites are fun to make and are sure to be the stars of your next St Patty's Day party!

- 1-1/2 cups butter, softened
- 1-1/2 cups sugar
- 2 eggs
- 3 teaspoons vanilla extract
- 4 cups all-purpose flour
- 1 teaspoon baking soda
- 1 teaspoon cream of tartar
- 1 teaspoon salt

ICING:

- 3-3/4 to 4 cups confectioners' sugar
- 3 tablespoons meringue powder
- 5 to 6 tablespoons warm water

Assorted paste food coloring

Green shimmer dust *or* edible glitter, optional

Green shamrock sprinkles, optional

Miniature semisweet chocolate chips

- In a large bowl, cream butter and sugar until light and fluffy. Add eggs, one at a time, beating well after each addition. Beat in vanilla. Combine the flour, baking soda, cream of tartar and salt; gradually add to the creamed mixture. Cover and refrigerate for 30 minutes or until easy to handle.

- On a lightly floured surface, roll out dough to 1/4-in. thickness. For leprechauns, cut out dough with lightly floured 5-in. gingerbread boy cookie cutter. If desired, trim leprechaun's body for a thinner shape.

- For each hat, cut a 1-1/2-in. square and a 1-3/4-in. x 1/4-in. brim from dough scraps. Place leprechauns 2 in. apart on ungreased baking sheets. Place hat squares and brims above heads, shaping gently to touch the heads.

- Bake at 350° for 10-14 minutes or until the edges are lightly browned. Cool for 1 minute before carefully removing to wire racks to cool completely.

- For icing, in a large bowl, combine the confectioners' sugar, meringue powder and water. Beat on high speed with a portable mixer for 10-12 minutes or on low speed with a stand mixer for 7-10 minutes or until peaks form.

- Tint small amounts of icing red, yellow and black. Leave a small amount plain. Tint remaining icing green and orange. Frost leprechauns; decorate with shimmer dust and shamrock sprinkles if desired. For eyes, attach miniature chocolate chips with plain frosting.

YIELD: ABOUT 3 DOZEN.

EDITOR'S NOTE: Edible glitter is available from Wilton Industries. Call 1-800/794-5866 or visit *www.wilton.com.*

caramel pecan shortbread

PREP 30 min. + chilling
BAKE 15 min. + cooling

DOROTHY BUITER • WORTH, ILLINOIS

My grandchildren love these sweet treats. I recommend doubling the recipe because they go fast.

- 3/4 cup butter, softened
- 3/4 cup confectioners' sugar
- 2 tablespoons evaporated milk
- 1 teaspoon vanilla extract
- 2 cups all-purpose flour
- 1/4 teaspoon salt

FILLING:

- 28 caramels
- 6 tablespoons evaporated milk
- 2 tablespoons butter
- 1/2 cup confectioners' sugar
- 3/4 cup finely chopped pecans

ICING:

- 1 cup (6 ounces) semisweet chocolate chips
- 3 tablespoons evaporated milk
- 2 tablespoons butter
- 1/2 cup confectioners' sugar
- 1/2 teaspoon vanilla extract

Pecan halves

- In a large bowl, cream butter and confectioners' sugar until light and fluffy. Beat in milk and vanilla. Combine flour and salt; gradually add to creamed mixture. Cover and refrigerate for 1 hour or until easy to handle.

- On a lightly floured surface, roll out the dough to 1/4-in. thickness. Cut into 2-in. x 1-in. strips. Place the strips 1 in. apart on greased baking sheets.

- Bake at 325° for 12-14 minutes or until lightly browned. Remove to wire racks to cool.

- For filling, combine the caramels and milk in a large saucepan. Cook and stir over medium-low heat until caramels are melted and smooth. Remove from the heat; stir in the butter, sugar and pecans. Cool for 5 minutes. Spread 1 teaspoon over each cookie.

- For icing, in a microwave, melt chips and milk; stir until smooth. Stir in the butter, sugar and vanilla. Cool for 5 minutes. Spread 1 teaspoon icing on each cookie; top each with a pecan half. Let stand until set. Store in an airtight container.

YIELD: ABOUT 4 DOZEN.

CARAMEL PECAN SHORTBREAD

STAR COOKIES

star cookies

PREP 45 min.
BAKE 10 min. + cooling

TASTE OF HOME TEST KITCHEN

A melted hard-candy center looks like stained glass surrounded by a delicious frosted cutout cookie in these eye-fetching snacks. Decorate them to match the season.

- 1-1/2 cups butter, softened
- 1-1/2 cups sugar
-    2 eggs
-    3 teaspoons vanilla extract
- 4-1/2 cups all-purpose flour
-    1 teaspoon baking soda
-    1 teaspoon cream of tartar
-    1 teaspoon salt
- Assorted colors of Jolly Rancher hard candies
-    1 tablespoon meringue powder
-    3 tablespoons plus 1/2 teaspoon water
- 2-2/3 cups confectioners' sugar
- Assorted colors of paste food coloring
- White edible glitter

• In a large bowl, cream butter and sugar until light and fluffy. Add eggs, one at a time, beating well after each addition. Beat in vanilla. Combine the flour, baking soda, cream of tartar and salt; gradually add to the creamed mixture. Divide into three portions; cover and refrigerate for 30 minutes or until easy to handle.

• Roll out one portion between two pieces of parchment paper to 1/4-in. thickness. Cut with a floured 5-in. star-shaped cookie cutter. Cut out centers with a 2-1/2-in. star-shaped cookie cutter. Place larger cutouts 2 in. apart on parchment-lined baking sheets. Repeat steps with the remaining dough; reroll small cutouts if desired.

• Place the same color of hard candies into small resealable plastic bags; crush candies. Sprinkle in center of each. Bake at 350° for 8-10 minutes or until lightly browned. Cool for 2-3 minutes or until candies are set before carefully removing to wire racks.

• In a small bowl, beat meringue powder and water until soft peaks form. Gradually add the confectioners' sugar. Tint icing to match the selected candies. Decorate cookies with icing; sprinkle with edible glitter.

YIELD: ABOUT 2 DOZEN.

chocolate lebkuchen

PREP 1 hour + cooling
BAKE 15 min. + cooling

CATHY LEMMON • ROYSE CITY, TEXAS

Having lived in Germany, I try to keep my German cooking and baking as authentic as possible. These lovely lebkuchen are a culinary Christmas custom.

- 1 cup plus 2 tablespoons all-purpose flour
- 1/4 cup sugar

Dash salt

- 1/3 cup cold butter, cubed
-    3 tablespoons water
-    1 teaspoon vanilla extract

TOPPING:

- 1/4 cup butter, softened
- 1/4 cup sugar
-    1 egg
-    1 tablespoon canola oil
- 2/3 cup quick-cooking oats
- 1/2 cup all-purpose flour
- 1/3 cup ground almonds
- 1/3 cup ground hazelnuts
- 1/4 cup baking cocoa
-    1 teaspoon baking powder
- 1/2 teaspoon ground cinnamon
- 1/4 teaspoon *each* ground cloves, cardamom and allspice
- 1/4 cup finely chopped candied lemon peel
- 1/4 cup finely chopped candied orange peel

GLAZE:

-    6 ounces semisweet chocolate, chopped
-    2 ounces unsweetened chocolate, chopped
- 1/4 cup butter, cubed

• In a small bowl, combine the flour, sugar and salt; cut in butter until mixture resembles coarse crumbs. Combine water and vanilla; gradually add to crumb mixture, tossing with a fork until dough forms a ball.

• On a lightly floured surface, roll out dough to 1/16-in. thickness. Cut with a floured 2-1/2-in. round cookie cutter. Place on ungreased baking sheets. Bake at 325° for 8-10 minutes or until set. Remove cookies from pans to wire racks to cool.

tip

lebkuchen

Lebkuchen is a traditional German cookie served at Christmas. It was created by monks in Franconia in the 13th century and has a flavor similar to gingerbread. The treats range in taste from spicy to sweet and come in a variety of shapes with round being the most popular. Ingredients may include spices such as aniseed, coriander, cloves, ginger, cardamom or allspice; nuts such as almonds, hazelnuts or walnuts; and candied fruit.

• For topping, in a small bowl, cream butter and sugar until light and fluffy. Beat in egg and oil. Combine the oats, flour, nuts, cocoa, baking powder and spices; gradually add to creamed mixture and mix well. Fold in candied peels.

• Drop a rounded tablespoonful of topping on each cookie; gently press down. Place 2 in. apart on ungreased baking sheets. Bake at 325° for 13-16 minutes or until set. Remove from pans to wire racks to cool.

• In a microwave-safe bowl, melt chocolate and butter; stir until smooth. Dip each cookie halfway in chocolate; allow the excess to drip off. Place on waxed paper; let stand until set. Store in an airtight container.

YIELD: ABOUT 1-1/2 DOZEN.

pastel tea cookies

PREP 1 hour + chilling
BAKE 10 min. + standing

LORI HENRY • ELKHART, INDIANA

These glazed cookies are perfect for nibbling between sips of coffee or tea at a luncheon or shower.

- 1 cup butter, softened
- 2/3 cup sugar
- 1 egg
- 1 teaspoon vanilla extract
- 2-1/2 cups all-purpose flour
- 1/2 teaspoon salt
- 1-1/4 cups confectioners' sugar
- 2 teaspoons meringue powder
- 5 teaspoons water
- Pastel food coloring

• In a large bowl, cream butter and sugar until light and fluffy. Beat in egg and vanilla. Combine flour and salt; gradually add to the creamed mixture. Cover and refrigerate for 1-2 hours or until the dough is easy to handle.

• On a lightly floured surface, roll out dough to 1/8-in. thickness. Cut with floured 2-1/2-in. butterfly or flower cookie cutters. Place 1 in. apart on ungreased baking sheets.

• Bake at 350° for 8-10 minutes or until the edges are lightly browned. Remove to wire racks to cool.

• For the glaze, in a small bowl, combine the confectioners' sugar and meringue powder; stir in water until smooth. Divide among small bowls; tint pastel colors. Spread over cookies; let stand until set.

YIELD: 4 DOZEN.

EDITOR'S NOTE: Meringue powder is available from Wilton Industries. Call 1-800/794-5866 or visit www.wilton.com.

PASTEL TEA COOKIES

SOFT MOLASSES CUTOUT COOKIES

soft molasses cutout cookies

PREP 20 min. + chilling
BAKE 10 min.

VIVIAN PERSON • BALATON, MINNESOTA

I received this recipe years ago, when my husband and I managed a retirement home. We'd always put out homemade goodies for morning and afternoon coffee, and these were the first to disappear.

- 1 cup shortening
- 1/2 cup sugar
- 1/2 cup packed brown sugar
- 2 eggs
- 1 cup dark molasses
- 5-1/2 cups all-purpose flour
- 3 teaspoons baking soda
- 1 teaspoon ground ginger
- 1 teaspoon ground cinnamon
- 3/4 teaspoon salt
- 1/2 cup water
- Frosting or confectioners' sugar, optional

• In a large bowl, cream shortening and sugars until light and fluffy. Add eggs, one at a time, beating well after each addition. Beat in molasses. Combine the flour, baking soda, ginger, cinnamon and salt; add to the creamed mixture alternately with water, beating well after each addition. Cover and refrigerate for 3 hours or until easy to handle.

• On a lightly floured surface, roll out dough to 1/4-in. thickness. Cut with 2-1/2-in. cookie cutters dipped in flour. Place 1 in. apart on greased baking sheets.

• Bake at 350° for 8-10 minutes or until edges are firm. Remove to wire racks to cool. Frost or dust with confectioners' sugar if desired.

YIELD: ABOUT 6-1/2 DOZEN.

sandwich cookies

The only thing better than one cookie is two cookies with a creamy filling in between them. These delights are tasty and easy to assemble, too.

viennese cookies

PREP 35 min. + chilling
BAKE 10 min. + cooling

BEVERLY STIRRAT ● MISSION, BRITISH COLUMBIA

A Swedish friend shared this recipe with me many years ago. A chocolate glaze tops the tender cookies filled with apricot jam.

1-1/4 cups butter, softened
2/3 cup sugar
2-1/4 cups all-purpose flour
1-2/3 cups ground almonds
1 cup apricot jam
2 cups (12 ounces) semisweet chocolate chips
2 tablespoons shortening

● In a large bowl, cream butter and sugar until light and fluffy. Combine flour and ground almonds; gradually add to creamed mixture and mix well. Cover and refrigerate for 1 hour.

● On a lightly floured surface, roll dough to 1/4-in. thickness. Cut with a floured 2-1/4-in. round cookie cutter. Place 2 in. apart on ungreased baking sheets.

● Bake at 350° for 7-9 minutes or until edges are lightly browned. Remove to wire racks to cool completely.

● Spread the jam on the bottoms of half of the cookies; top with remaining cookies. In a microwave, melt the chocolate chips and shortening; stir until smooth. Dip half of each sandwich cookie into the chocolate mixture; allow excess to drip off. Place on waxed paper until set. Store in an airtight container.

YIELD: ABOUT 3 DOZEN.

WHOOPIE PIES

VIENNESE COOKIES

whoopie pies

PREP 15 min.
BAKE 5 min. + cooling

RUTH ANN STELFOX ● RAYMOND, ALBERTA

These ooey-gooey confections feature an irresistible cream filling sandwiched between two chocolate cupcake-like cookies. Enlist the kids to help assemble these old-fashioned favorites.

1 cup butter, softened
1-1/2 cups sugar
2 eggs
2 teaspoons vanilla extract
4 cups all-purpose flour
3/4 cup baking cocoa
2 teaspoons baking soda
1/2 teaspoon salt
1 cup water
1 cup buttermilk

FILLING:

2 cups confectioners' sugar
2 cups marshmallow creme
1/2 cup butter, softened
2 teaspoons vanilla extract

● In a large bowl, cream butter and sugar until light and fluffy. Add eggs and vanilla; mix well. Combine the flour, cocoa, baking soda and salt; add to creamed mixture alternately with water and buttermilk, beating well after each addition.

● Drop dough by tablespoonfuls 2 in. apart onto greased baking sheets. Bake at 375° for 5-7 minutes or until set. Remove to wire racks to cool completely.

● In a small bowl, beat filling ingredients until fluffy. Spread on the bottoms of half of the cookies; top with remaining cookies.

YIELD: 1-1/2 DOZEN.

colorful peanut butter crackers

PREP 35 min. + chilling

RUTH CASSIS ● UNIVERSITY PLACE, WASHINGTON

Bring these sweet-and-salty treats to your next bake sale or potluck. Add any cake decorator shapes to suit the season.

    4 ounces cream cheese, cubed
  1/2 cup creamy peanut butter
  1/4 cup honey
   48 butter-flavored crackers
    2 cups (12 ounces) semisweet chocolate chips
    4 teaspoons shortening
  1/4 cup 2% milk
Cake decorator holiday shapes

● In a microwave-safe bowl, heat cream cheese on high for 15 seconds or until very soft. Add peanut butter and honey; stir until smooth. Spread over half of the crackers; top with remaining crackers.

● In a microwave, melt chocolate chips and shortening; stir until smooth. Heat milk; stir into chocolate mixture.

● Dip each cracker sandwich in the chocolate mixture, allowing excess to drip off. Place on waxed paper-lined baking sheets; decorate as desired. Refrigerate cookies for 45 minutes or until set.

YIELD: 2 DOZEN.

EDITOR'S NOTE: This recipe was tested in a 1,100-watt microwave.

ICE CREAM SANDWICHES

COLORFUL PEANUT BUTTER CRACKERS

ice cream sandwiches

PREP 20 min.

BAKE 10 min. + freezing

TASTE OF HOME TEST KITCHEN

Our Test Kitchen experts created these chilly treats perfect for hot, sunny days. The gluten-free chocolate cookie is so tasty you could eat it plain...but you won't want to miss out on the ice cream!

  1/3 cup butter, softened
  1/2 cup sugar
    2 tablespoons beaten egg
  1/2 teaspoon vanilla extract
  2/3 cup white rice flour
  1/4 cup potato starch
  1/4 cup baking cocoa
    2 tablespoons tapioca flour
  1/2 teaspoon baking powder
  1/2 teaspoon baking soda
  1/2 teaspoon xanthan gum
  1/8 teaspoon salt
1-1/2 cups vanilla ice cream, softened

● In a small bowl, cream butter and sugar. Beat in egg and vanilla. Combine the rice flour, starch, cocoa, tapioca flour, baking powder, baking soda, xanthan gum and salt; add to creamed mixture and mix well.

● Drop by rounded tablespoonfuls 2 in. apart onto a baking sheet coated with cooking spray, forming 12 cookies; flatten slightly. Bake at 350° for 8-10 minutes or until set. Remove to a wire rack to cool completely.

● Spread 1/4 cup ice cream on the bottoms of half of the cookies; top with remaining cookies. Wrap each in plastic wrap. Freeze for 3 hours or until firm.

YIELD: 1/2 DOZEN.

EDITOR'S NOTE: Read all ingredient labels for possible gluten content prior to use. Ingredient formulas can change, and production facilities vary among brands. If you're concerned that your brand may contain gluten, contact the manufacturer.

peanut butter 'n' jelly cookies

PREP 15 min. + chilling

BAKE 10 min. + cooling

MARGARET WILSON ● SUN CITY, CALIFORNIA

The classic combination of peanut butter and jelly makes a scrumptious sandwich cookie. Both children and adults enjoy these snacks.

- 1/2 cup shortening
- 1/2 cup peanut butter
- 1/2 cup sugar
- 1/2 cup packed brown sugar
- 1 egg
- 1-1/4 cups all-purpose flour
- 3/4 teaspoon baking soda
- 1/2 teaspoon baking powder
- 1/4 teaspoon salt

Jam *or* jelly

- In a bowl, cream shortening, peanut butter and sugars. Beat in the egg. Combine the dry ingredients; gradually add to creamed mixture. Cover dough and chill for 1 hour. Roll into 1-in. balls; place 2 in. apart on greased baking sheets. Flatten slightly.

- Bake at 375° for 10 minutes or until golden brown. Cool on wire racks. Spread jam on the bottom of half of the cookies; top with remaining cookies.

YIELD: ABOUT 4-1/2 DOZEN.

maple sandwich cookies

PREP 15 min.
BAKE 10 min. + cooling

BARBARA SCACCHI • LIMESTONE, NEW YORK

My mom loves maple flavoring, so I created this recipe just for her. But the whole family loves these tasty cookies.

- 1 cup butter, softened
- 3/4 cup packed brown sugar
- 1 egg yolk
- 2 cups all-purpose flour

Sugar

FILLING:

- 1-1/4 cups confectioners' sugar
- 2 tablespoons 2% milk
- 2 tablespoons butter, softened
- 1/2 teaspoon maple flavoring

- In a large bowl, cream the butter and brown sugar until light and fluffy. Beat in egg yolk. Gradually add flour and mix well.

- Shape into 1-in. balls. Dip the tops in sugar. Place sugar side up 2 in. apart on ungreased baking sheets. Flatten with a fork.

- Bake at 325° for 10-12 minutes or until golden brown. Remove to wire racks to cool.

- In a small bowl, beat the filling ingredients until smooth. Spread on the bottoms of half of the cookies; top with remaining cookies.

YIELD: ABOUT 3 DOZEN.

hazelnut-espresso sandwich cookies

PREP 45 min. + chilling
BAKE 10 min. + cooling

CINDY BEBERMAN • ORLAND PARK, ILLINOIS

The inspiration for this cute cookie came from my sister's description of a hazelnut cookie she tried in Italy. She declared my version to be a wonderful approximation. My kids like to help fill them.

- 1 cup butter, softened
- 1-1/4 cups sugar
- 1 egg
- 1 egg yolk
- 4 teaspoons instant espresso granules
- 2 teaspoons vanilla extract
- 2-1/2 cups all-purpose flour
- 1/2 teaspoon salt
- 1/2 teaspoon baking powder
- 1 cup finely ground hazelnuts

FILLING:

- 1-3/4 cups semisweet chocolate chips, *divided*
- 1-1/4 cups milk chocolate chips
- 1 cup heavy whipping cream

- In a large bowl, cream butter and sugar until light and fluffy. Beat in the egg, yolk, espresso granules and vanilla. Combine the flour, salt and baking powder; gradually add to creamed mixture and mix well. Stir in hazelnuts.

- Divide dough into thirds; flatten each portion into a circle. Wrap each in plastic wrap; refrigerate for 1 hour or until easy to handle.

- On a lightly floured surface, roll out one portion of the dough to 1/8-in. thickness. Cut with a floured 1-1/2-in. cookie cutter; place 1/2 in. apart on ungreased baking sheets. Repeat with remaining dough; chill and reroll scraps.

- Bake at 375° for 6-8 minutes or until edges begin to brown. Remove to wire racks to cool.

- For filling, place 3/4 cup semisweet chocolate chips and milk chocolate chips in a small bowl. In a small saucepan, bring cream just to a boil. Pour over the chocolate; whisk until smooth. Refrigerate for 1-1/2 hours or until filling reaches spreading consistency, stirring occasionally.

- Spread filling over the bottom of half of the cookies; top with remaining cookies. In a microwave, melt remaining semisweet chips; stir until smooth. Drizzle over cookies. Let stand until set. Store in an airtight container in the refrigerator.

YIELD: 3 DOZEN.

HAZELNUT-ESPRESSO SANDWICH COOKIES

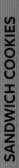

CHOCOLATE-MINT SANDWICH COOKIES

chocolate-mint sandwich cookies

PREP 25 min. + chilling
BAKE 10 min.

MONICA KNEUER • PECONIC, NEW YORK

A creamy and refreshing mint filling sandwiched between two chocolate cookies makes for some tasty nibbling.

>   3/4 cup butter, softened
>   1 cup sugar
>   1 egg
>   1/2 teaspoon vanilla extract
>   2 cups all-purpose flour
>   3/4 cup baking cocoa
>   1 teaspoon baking powder
>   1/2 teaspoon baking soda
>   1/2 teaspoon salt
>   1/4 cup 2% milk

FILLING:

>   3 tablespoons butter, softened
>   1-1/2 cups confectioners' sugar
>   1 tablespoon 2% milk
>   1/4 teaspoon peppermint extract
>   2 to 3 drops green food coloring, optional

- In a large bowl, cream butter and sugar until light and fluffy. Beat in egg and vanilla. Combine the flour, cocoa, baking powder, baking soda and salt; gradually add to creamed mixture alternately with milk, beating well after each addition. Shape into two 10-1/2-in. rolls; wrap each in plastic wrap. Refrigerate overnight.

- Unwrap the dough and cut into 1/8-in. slices. Place 2 in. apart onto lightly greased baking sheets. Bake at 325° for 9-11 minutes or until edges are set. Remove to wire racks to cool.

- Combine the filling ingredients; beat until smooth. Add food coloring if desired. Spread on the bottom of half of the cookies; top with remaining cookies.

YIELD: 5 DOZEN.

lemon snowdrops

PREP 30 min.
BAKE 10 min.

BERNICE MARTINONI • PETALUMA, CALIFORNIA

This crispy cookie with a luscious filling is impossible to resist!

>   1 cup butter, softened
>   1/2 cup confectioners' sugar
>   1 teaspoon lemon extract
>   2 cups all-purpose flour
>   1/4 teaspoon salt

LEMON BUTTER FILLING:

>   1 egg, lightly beaten
>   2/3 cup sugar
>   3 tablespoons lemon juice
>   Grated peel of 1 lemon
>   4-1/2 teaspoons butter, softened
>   Additional confectioners' sugar

- In a small bowl, cream butter and sugar until light and fluffy. Beat in extract. Combine flour and salt; gradually add to creamed mixture and mix well.

- Roll teaspoonfuls of dough into balls. Place 1 in. apart on ungreased baking sheets; flatten slightly. Bake at 350° for 10-12 minutes or until lightly browned.

- Meanwhile, for filling, combine egg, sugar, lemon juice, peel and butter in a heavy saucepan. Cook and stir until thickened and a thermometer reads 160°, about 20 minutes. Refrigerate for 1 hour or until completely cooled.

- Spread the lemon filling on the bottoms of half of the cookies; top with the remaining cookies and roll in additional confectioners' sugar. Store in the refrigerator.

YIELD: ABOUT 4 DOZEN.

oatmeal sandwich cremes

PREP 20 min.
BAKE 15 min. + cooling

LESLEY MANSFIELD
MONROE, NORTH CAROLINA

These hearty cookies appeal to all palates whenever I take them to a family get-together or church bake sale. The creamy filling sandwiched between two tender oatmeal cookies is well worth the little extra effort they require.

>   3/4 cup shortening
>   1 cup sugar
>   1 cup packed brown sugar
>   1 egg
>   1/4 cup water
>   1 teaspoon vanilla extract
>   1-1/2 cups self-rising flour
>   1 teaspoon baking soda
>   1 teaspoon ground cinnamon
>   3 cups quick-cooking oats
>   3/4 cup raisins

FILLING:

>   1/2 cup butter, softened
>   1/2 cup shortening
>   3-3/4 cups confectioners' sugar
>   2 tablespoons 2% milk
>   1 teaspoon vanilla extract
>   Dash salt

- In a large bowl, cream shortening and sugars until light and fluffy. Beat in the egg, water and vanilla. Combine the flour, baking soda and cinnamon; gradually add to creamed mixture and mix well. Stir in oats and raisins.

- Drop dough by tablespoonfuls 3 in. apart on ungreased baking sheets. Flatten with a glass. Bake at 325° for 13-14 minutes or until lightly browned. Remove to wire racks to cool.

- In a large bowl, combine filling ingredients; beat until smooth. Spread on bottoms of half of the cookies; top with remaining cookies.

YIELD: 3 DOZEN.

EDITOR'S NOTE: As a substitute for each cup of self-rising flour, place 1-1/2 teaspoons baking powder and 1/2 teaspoon salt in a measuring cup. Add all-purpose flour to measure 1 cup.

tip

tasty substitutions

To make Oatmeal Sandwich Cremes even more yummy, add dried cranberries or chocolate-covered raisins in place of the plain raisins. Another fun substitution to try, especially in fall, is to replace the cinnamon with pumpkin pie spice or apple pie spice. The cookies will taste extra-special, and your house will smell heavenly while they're baking in the oven.

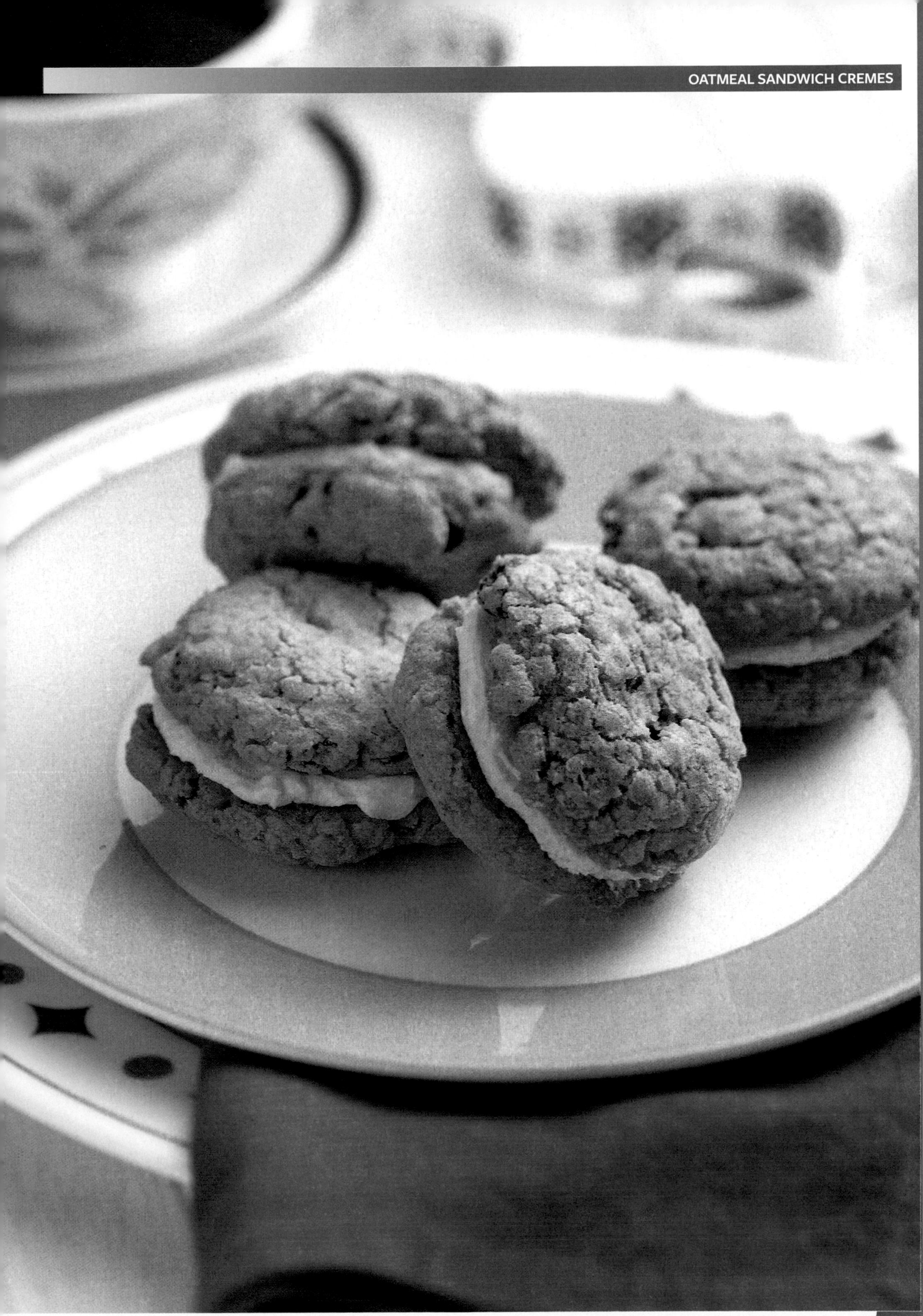

CHOCOLATE SANDWICH COOKIES

chocolate sandwich cookies

PREP 25 min.
BAKE 10 min.

ANNE FRIESEN • MORDEN, MANITOBA

My five children love having these yummy cookies packed in their lunch boxes and keep asking when I'll make them next. The recipe comes from a family cookbook that was put together for one of our annual reunions.

- 1 cup butter, softened
- 2 cups sugar
- 2 eggs
- 1/2 cup heavy whipping cream
- 1 teaspoon vanilla extract
- 3 cups quick-cooking *or* rolled oats
- 1-3/4 cups all-purpose flour
- 1/2 cup baking cocoa
- 1 teaspoon baking powder
- 1 teaspoon baking soda
- 1/4 teaspoon salt

FILLING:

- 2 tablespoons cornstarch
- 2 tablespoons baking cocoa
- 3/4 cup water
- 1/2 cup sugar
- 2 tablespoons butter
- 1/2 teaspoon vanilla extract

- In a large bowl, cream butter and sugar until light and fluffy. Beat in the eggs, cream and vanilla. Combine the dry ingredients; gradually add to creamed mixture and mix well.

- Drop by tablespoonfuls onto lightly greased baking sheets. Bake at 350° for 10 minutes or until set. Cool on wire racks.

- Meanwhile, in a small saucepan, combine the cornstarch, cocoa and water until smooth. Stir in sugar and butter. Bring to a boil over medium heat; cook and stir for 2 minutes or until thickened. Remove from the heat; stir in vanilla. Cool. Spread on the bottoms of half of the cookies; top with remaining cookies.

YIELD: 2 DOZEN.

chocolate peanut grahams

PREP 10 min. + chilling

TASTE OF HOME TEST KITCHEN

Cinnamon graham crackers are the base for this tasty chocolate treat.

- 4 whole cinnamon graham crackers, broken into quarters
- 1/4 cup creamy peanut butter
- 1 cup (6 ounces) semisweet chocolate chips
- 3 teaspoons shortening

- Spread half of the graham cracker quarters with peanut butter; top with remaining crackers.

- In a microwave-safe bowl, melt chocolate chips and shortening; stir until smooth. Dip the crackers into chocolate; place on a waxed paper-lined pan. Refrigerate until set.

YIELD: 1-1/4 DOZEN.

sam's chocolate sandwich cookies

PREP 30 min.
BAKE 10 min. + cooling

SALVATORE BERTOLINO
INDIANA, PENNSYLVANIA

These soft, not-too-sweet chocolate cookies have a heavenly cream filling. Kids and adults alike will devour them!

- 1 cup shortening
- 2 cups sugar
- 2 eggs
- 1 cup (8 ounces) sour cream
- 1 cup hot brewed coffee
- 1 teaspoon vanilla extract
- 4 cups all-purpose flour
- 3/4 cup baking cocoa
- 2 teaspoons baking soda
- 1/2 teaspoon baking powder

FILLING:

- 1/4 cup all-purpose flour
- 3/4 cup 2% milk
- 1 cup shortening
- 2 cups confectioners' sugar
- 2 teaspoons vanilla extract
- 1/8 teaspoon salt

- In a large bowl, cream shortening and sugar until light and fluffy. Add eggs, one at a time, beating well after each addition. Beat in the sour cream, coffee and vanilla. Combine the dry ingredients; gradually add to the creamed mixture and mix well.

- Drop by tablespoonfuls 2 in. apart onto greased baking sheets. Bake at 350° for 9-11 minutes or until firm to touch. Remove to wire racks to cool.

- In a small saucepan, combine flour and milk until smooth. Bring to a boil; cook and stir for 2 minutes or until thickened. Cool to room temperature, about 20 minutes. In a large bowl, beat shortening, confectioners' sugar, vanilla and salt until smooth. Add milk mixture; beat until light and fluffy.

- Spread 2 teaspoonfuls of filling on the bottom of half of the cookies; top with remaining cookies.

YIELD: ABOUT 4 DOZEN.

ginger creme sandwich cookies

PREP 25 min. + chilling
BAKE 10 min. + cooling

CAROL WALSTON • GRANBURY, TEXAS

With a lemony filling, these spiced cookies go over big because they have old-fashioned, comfort-food appeal. Your party guests will snatch them up.

- 3/4 cup shortening
- 1 cup packed light brown sugar
- 1 egg
- 1/4 cup molasses
- 2-1/4 cups all-purpose flour
- 3 teaspoons ground ginger
- 2 teaspoons baking soda
- 1 teaspoon ground cinnamon
- 1/2 teaspoon salt
- 1/4 cup sugar

FILLING:
- 1 package (3 ounces) cream cheese, softened
- 1/3 cup butter, softened
- 2 teaspoons lemon extract
- 2 cups confectioners' sugar
- 1 teaspoon vanilla extract

- In a large bowl, cream the shortening and brown sugar until light and fluffy. Beat in egg and molasses. Combine the flour, ginger, baking soda, cinnamon and salt; gradually add to creamed mixture and mix well. Cover and refrigerate overnight.

- Shape into 1-in. balls; roll in sugar. Place 2 in. apart on ungreased baking sheets. Flatten with a fork, forming a crisscross pattern. Bake at 375° for 8-10 minutes or until set (do not overbake). Remove to wire racks to cool.

- In a small bowl, combine filling ingredients until smooth. Spread over the bottoms of half of the cookies; top with remaining cookies. Store in the refrigerator.

YIELD: 2-1/2 DOZEN.

CAP AND BALL COOKIES

cap and ball cookies

PREP 40 min. + standing

TASTE OF HOME TEST KITCHEN

You'll have a ball decorating plain packaged cookies to create these clever confections that look like baseballs and team caps.

- 2 cups white baking chips
- 1 tablespoon shortening
- 16 cream-filled chocolate sandwich cookies
- 1 tube red decorating frosting
- 1 package (12 ounces) chocolate and marshmallow cookies
- 12 chocolate wafer cookies
- 12 red M&M's

- In a microwave or heavy saucepan, melt chips and shortening; stir until smooth. Dip sandwich cookies into mixture and allow excess to drip off; place on waxed paper to harden.

- Meanwhile, spread the red frosting over half of the bottom of each marshmallow cookie; press off-center onto a chocolate wafer to create a cap.

- Pipe a line of frosting where the cookies meet. Pipe stitch marks down the sides of marshmallow cookies. Attach an M&M on top with a dab of frosting.

- On the dipped sandwich cookies, pipe stitch marks to create baseballs.

YIELD: 16 BASEBALLS AND 12 CAPS.

EDITOR'S NOTE: This recipe was tested with Nabisco Pinwheels.

GINGER CREME SANDWICH COOKIES

BROWNED-BUTTER SANDWICH SPRITZ

browned-butter sandwich spritz

PREP 50 min. + chilling
BAKE 10 min. + cooling

DEIRDRE DEE COX ● MILWAUKEE, WISCONSIN

A heavenly sweet maple filling makes these scrumptious spritz cookies stand apart from the rest. You can count on them to come out buttery and tender. They're almost too pretty to eat.

- 1 cup plus 2 tablespoons butter, cubed
- 1-1/4 cups confectioners' sugar, *divided*
- 1 egg
- 1 egg yolk
- 2 teaspoons vanilla extract
- 2-1/4 cups all-purpose flour
- 1/2 teaspoon salt
- 1/2 cup maple syrup

● In a small heavy saucepan, cook and stir butter over medium heat for 8-10 minutes or until golden brown. Transfer to a small bowl; refrigerate until firm, about 1 hour.

● Set aside 2 tablespoons browned butter for filling. In a large bowl, beat 1/2 cup confectioners' sugar and remaining browned butter until smooth. Beat in the egg, yolk and vanilla. Combine flour and salt; gradually add to creamed mixture and mix well.

● Using a cookie press fitted with the disk of your choice, press dough 2 in. apart onto parchment paper-lined baking sheets. Bake at 375° for 8-9 minutes or until set (do not brown). Remove to wire racks to cool.

● In a small heavy saucepan, bring the syrup to a boil. Cool slightly. Whisk in remaining confectioners' sugar until smooth. Beat the reserved browned butter until light and fluffy. Beat in syrup mixture until smooth.

● Spread 1 teaspoon of filling over the bottom of half of the cookies. Top with remaining cookies.

YIELD: ABOUT 3 DOZEN.

frozen sandwich cookies

PREP 30 min.

MARY ANN GOMEZ ● LOMBARD, ILLINOIS

These cool, creamy treats are perfect for a hot, humid day. And with just three simple ingredients, they're a snap to make.

- 1/2 cup spreadable strawberry cream cheese
- 1/4 cup strawberry yogurt
- 16 chocolate wafers

● In a small bowl, beat the cream cheese and yogurt until smooth. Spread mixture on the bottom of half of the chocolate wafers; top with remaining wafers. Place cookies on a baking sheet. Cover and freeze for 25 minutes.

● Serve or wrap in plastic wrap and store in the freezer.

YIELD: 1-1/4 DOZEN.

chocolate almond cookies

PREP 15 min. + chilling
BAKE 10 min. + cooling

KATHRYN WERNER ● PETERBOROUGH, ONTARIO

Special occasions around our house have always been enjoyed with these chocolate-dipped, jam-filled cookies. They not only look appealing, they taste terrific, too. You can use any jam that suits your taste.

- 1/2 cup butter, softened
- 6 tablespoons sugar
- 1-1/2 teaspoons vanilla extract
- 1 cup all-purpose flour
- 1 cup finely chopped blanched almonds

FROZEN SANDWICH COOKIES

1/4 to 1/2 cup raspberry jam *or* jam of your choice

3 ounces semisweet chocolate, melted

• In a large bowl, cream the butter, sugar and vanilla until light and fluffy. Combine flour and almonds; gradually add to the creamed mixture. Shape into one 12-in. roll; wrap in plastic wrap. Refrigerate for 4 hours or until firm.

• Unwrap; cut into 1/4-in. slices. Place 2 in. apart on ungreased baking sheets. Bake at 350° for 8-10 minutes or until lightly browned. Remove to wire racks to cool.

• Spread 1 teaspoon jam on the bottom of half of the cookies; top with remaining cookies. Dip cookies halfway into melted chocolate; shake off excess. Place on waxed paper-lined baking sheets to set.

YIELD: 2 DOZEN.

beach ball ice cream sandwiches

PREP 35 min. + freezing

PATTIE ANN FORSSBERG • LOGAN, KANSAS

Who can resist creamy ice cream between homemade sugar cookies? These treats are the perfect way to celebrate a beach vacation or the start of summer.

3 tablespoons butter, softened
1-1/2 cups confectioners' sugar
1/2 teaspoon vanilla extract
1 to 2 tablespoons 2% milk
Red, blue, yellow and green food coloring
48 round sugar cookies
1 quart vanilla ice cream, softened

• In a small bowl, combine the butter, confectioners' sugar, vanilla and enough milk to achieve spreading consistency. Divide frosting among five bowls; tint each a different color with red, blue, yellow and green food coloring. Leave one plain.

• Frost tops of 24 sugar cookies with colored frostings to resemble beach balls. Let frosting dry completely.

• Spoon the ice cream onto bottom of plain cookies; top with the frosted cookies. Place in individual plastic bags; seal. Freeze cookies until serving.

YIELD: 2 DOZEN.

CARAMEL CREAMS

caramel creams

PREP 20 min. + chilling
BAKE 15 min. + cooling

BARBARA YOUNGERS • KINGMAN, KANSAS

These cookies are delicious plain, but I like to make them into sandwich cookies with the brown butter filling. In a pinch, use canned frosting instead of making your own from scratch.

1 cup butter, softened
2/3 cup packed brown sugar
2 egg yolks
1/2 teaspoon vanilla extract
2-1/2 cups all-purpose flour
1/3 cup finely chopped pecans
1/4 teaspoon salt
FILLING:
2 tablespoons plus 1-1/2 teaspoons butter
1-1/2 cups confectioners' sugar
1/2 teaspoon vanilla extract
2 to 3 tablespoons heavy whipping cream

• In a large bowl, cream butter and brown sugar until light and fluffy. Beat in egg yolks and vanilla. Combine the flour, pecans and salt; gradually add to the creamed mixture and beat well. Shape into two 10-in. rolls; wrap each in plastic wrap. Refrigerate for 1-2 hours.

• Unwrap and cut into 1/4-in. slices. Place 2 in. apart on ungreased baking sheets. Bake at 350° for 11-13 minutes or until golden brown. Remove to wire racks to cool.

• For filling, in a small saucepan, cook butter over medium heat until golden brown. Pour into a large bowl, beat in the confectioners' sugar, vanilla and enough cream to achieve a spreading consistency. Spread filling on the bottom of half of the cookies; top with the remaining cookies.

YIELD: ABOUT 3 DOZEN.

COCONUT LEMON CRISPS

coconut lemon crisps

PREP 20 min.
BAKE 10 min. + cooling

SEGARIE MOODLEY • LONGWOOD, FLORIDA

We had these cookies at our wedding reception, where they brought smiles and compliments. They've become one of our anniversary dinner trademarks.

7 tablespoons butter, softened
1/4 cup sugar
1/2 teaspoon vanilla extract
1 cup all-purpose flour
1 egg white, beaten
1/2 cup flaked coconut

FILLING:

1/3 cup sugar
4-1/2 teaspoons cornstarch
3/4 cup water
1 egg yolk, beaten

3 tablespoons butter, softened
2 tablespoons lemon juice

- In a small bowl, cream the butter, sugar and vanilla until light and fluffy. Gradually add flour and mix well. On a lightly floured surface, roll out half of the dough to 1/8-in. thickness. Cut with a floured 2-in. round cookie cutter. Repeat with remaining dough, using a floured 2-in. doughnut cutter so the center is cut out of each cookie.

- Place 1 in. apart on lightly greased baking sheets. Brush egg white over cookies with cutout centers; sprinkle with coconut. Bake at 350° for 8-10 minutes. Remove to wire racks to cool.

- For filling, in a large saucepan, combine sugar and cornstarch; stir in water until smooth. Cook and stir over medium-high heat until thickened and bubbly. Reduce heat to low; cook and stir for 2 minutes longer. Remove from the heat. Stir a small amount of hot filling into egg yolk; return all to the pan, stirring constantly. Bring to a gentle boil; cook and stir for 2 minutes. Remove from the heat; gently stir in butter and lemon juice. Cool to room temperature without stirring.

- Spread one teaspoon of filling on the bottom of each solid cookie; place the coconut-topped cookie over lemon filling. Store in the refrigerator.

YIELD: 1-1/2 DOZEN.

mocha sandwich cookies

PREP 20 min. + chilling
BAKE 10 min. + cooling

ANNA SYLVESTER • SYLVANIA, OHIO

A cookie tray just isn't complete without these melt-in-your-mouth treats. The crisp, buttery shortbread complements the indulgent mocha filling.

3/4 cup butter, softened
1/2 cup confectioners' sugar
1 teaspoon vanilla extract
1 cup all-purpose flour
1/2 cup cornstarch

FILLING:

2 tablespoons butter, softened
2/3 cup confectioners' sugar
1-1/2 teaspoons heavy whipping cream
1/4 teaspoon almond extract
2 tablespoons baking cocoa
1/2 teaspoon instant coffee granules
1 to 2 tablespoons boiling water
2 tablespoons sliced almonds, toasted and finely chopped

- In a large bowl, cream butter and confectioners' sugar. Beat in vanilla. Combine flour and cornstarch; gradually add to creamed mixture and mix well. Cover and refrigerate for 1 hour.

- Shape dough into 3/4-in. balls; press lightly to flatten. Place 1 in. apart on ungreased baking sheets. Bake at 375° for 10-12 minutes. Cool on wire racks.

- For filling, in a small bowl, cream butter and confectioners' sugar. Beat in cream and extract. In a small bowl, combine the cocoa, coffee and boiling water; stir to dissolve coffee granules. Add to creamed mixture and mix well. Fold in almonds. Cover and refrigerate for 30 minutes.

- Spread filling over the bottom of half of the cookies; top with remaining cookies. Store in the refrigerator.

YIELD: 2 DOZEN.

cream wafers

PREP 25 min. + chilling
BAKE 10 min. + cooling

LINDA CLINKENBEARD • VINCENNES, INDIANA

My sons used to help me make these cookies, and now my oldest granddaughter helps. When the smaller grandchildren are home, they help, too. The cute little sandwich cookies are tender, buttery and unbelievably good!

- 1/2 cup butter, softened
- 1 cup all-purpose flour
- 3 tablespoons heavy whipping cream

Sugar

FILLING:

- 1/4 cup butter, softened
- 3/4 cup confectioners' sugar
- 1/2 teaspoon vanilla extract
- 1-1/2 to 2 teaspoons heavy whipping cream
- 1 drop *each* red and green food coloring

• In a small bowl, beat the butter, flour and cream. Cover and refrigerate for 1 hour or until easy to handle.

• On a lightly floured surface, roll out dough to 1/8-in. thickness. Cut with a floured 1-1/4-in. round cookie cutter. Place 1 in. apart on ungreased baking sheets. Sprinkle with sugar. Prick each cookie 3-4 times with a fork.

• Bake at 375° for 7-9 minutes or until set. Remove to wire racks to cool.

• In a small bowl, combine the butter, confectioners' sugar, vanilla and enough cream to achieve desired consistency. Remove half to another bowl; tint one portion of filling with red food coloring and the other half with green. Carefully spread filling on bottom of half of cookies; top with remaining cookies.

YIELD: 2 DOZEN.

CREAM WAFERS

PEANUT BUTTER S'MORES

peanut butter s'mores

PREP 10 min.

LILY JULOW • GAINESVILLE, FLORIDA

I turn to this recipe when I need something fun and easy for dessert. It's a decadent take on classic campfire s'mores.

- 8 large chocolate chip cookies
- 4 teaspoons hot fudge ice cream topping
- 4 large marshmallows
- 4 peanut butter cups

• Spread the bottoms of four cookies with fudge topping.

• Using a long-handled fork, grill marshmallows 6 in. from medium-hot heat until golden brown, turning occasionally. Carefully place a marshmallow and a peanut butter cup on each fudge-topped cookie; top with remaining cookies. Serve immediately.

YIELD: 4 COOKIE SANDWICHES.

marshmallows

Store marshmallows in the freezer to keep them from turning hard. Once thawed, they will be as soft as fresh marshmallows. To separate sticky marshmallows, place a spoonful of confectioners' sugar in the bag and shake it well.

cutout pumpkin sandwich cookies

PREP 40 min. + chilling
BAKE 10 min. + cooling

SCHELBY THOMPSON
CAMDEN WYOMING, DELAWARE

Apricot preserves peek out of these buttery, tender sugar cookies. Make them throughout the year with a variety of cookie cutter shapes.

    1   cup butter, softened
1-1/4   cups sugar, *divided*
    2   eggs, *separated*
2-1/2   cups all-purpose flour
  1/4   teaspoon salt
        Confectioners' sugar
  1/2   cup ground almonds
  3/4   cup apricot preserves

- In a large bowl, cream butter and 3/4 cup sugar until light and fluffy. Add egg yolks, one at a time, beating well after each addition. Combine flour and salt; gradually add to creamed mixture and mix well. Shape dough into a ball; chill for 1 hour or until firm.

- On a surface dusted with confectioners' sugar, roll dough to 1/8-in. thickness; cut with a 3-in. pumpkin-shaped cookie cutter. Cut a 1-1/2-in. pumpkin from the center of half the cookies and remove (set aside small pumpkin cutouts to bake separately).

- Place on greased baking sheets. Beat egg whites until frothy. Combine almonds and remaining sugar. Brush each cookie with egg whites; sprinkle with almond mixture. Bake at 350° for 6-8 minutes or until lightly browned. Immediately remove cookies to wire racks to cool completely.

- Spread 1-1/2 teaspoons of apricot preserves on the bottoms of the solid cookies; place cookies with cutout centers, almond side up, over filling.

YIELD: 2 DOZEN.

toffee sandwich cookies

PREP 20 min.
BAKE 10 min.

APRIL MCDAVID • CENTERBURG, OHIO

My brother's quest to find a filled toffee cookie inspired me to spend hours in the kitchen coming up with a winning combination. Of the 14 kinds of cookies I bake each Christmas, these morsels are the first to disappear!

CUTOUT PUMPKIN SANDWICH COOKIES

    1   cup butter, softened
    1   cup packed brown sugar
  1/2   cup sugar
    2   eggs
    2   teaspoons vanilla extract
2-1/2   cups all-purpose flour
  1/2   teaspoon baking soda
  1/4   teaspoon salt
    1   cup English toffee bits *or* almond brickle chips

FILLING:

  2/3   cup butter, softened
    4   cups confectioners' sugar
    1   teaspoon vanilla extract
    3   to 5 tablespoons half-and-half cream *or* milk

- In a large bowl, cream butter and sugars until light and fluffy. Add eggs, one at a time, beating well after each addition. Beat in vanilla. Combine the flour, baking soda and salt; gradually add to the creamed mixture and mix well. Stir in toffee bits (dough will be stiff).

- Drop by rounded teaspoonfuls 2 in. apart onto ungreased baking sheets. Bake at 350° for 10 minutes or until firm (do not brown).

- In a small bowl, beat the butter, sugar, vanilla and enough cream to achieve spreading consistency. Spread on the bottom of half of the cookies; top with remaining cookies.

YIELD: 4 DOZEN.

be-mine sandwich cookies

PREP 20 min.

DARCIE CROSS • NOVI, MICHIGAN

These simple sensations are the first thing to disappear at bake sales, potlucks and parties. They're cute, colorful and extremely fast to make.

    6   ounces white *or* milk chocolate candy coating, coarsely chopped
   50   to 55 chocolate cream-filled sandwich cookies
        Assorted candy sprinkles *or* decorations

- In a microwave, melt 2 oz. of candy coating at a time, stirring until smooth. Spread over cookie tops; decorate immediately. Place on waxed paper until set.

YIELD: ABOUT 4-1/2 DOZEN.

PEACHY COOKIES

peachy cookies

PREP 2-1/2 hours
BAKE 15 min. + standing

ANDREA CUTERI • CORAOPOLIS, PENNSYLVANIA

One look at these pretty pastries and you'll think they came fresh off the tree instead of the dessert tray. I bake them for holidays, weddings and any celebration that calls for a peach of a cookie!

- 2 eggs
- 1 cup sugar
- 3/4 cup canola oil
- 1/2 cup 2% milk
- 1/2 teaspoon vanilla extract
- 4 cups all-purpose flour
- 3/4 teaspoon baking powder

FILLING:
- 1 cup apricot preserves
- 1/2 cup finely chopped pecans
- 1 package (3 ounces) cream cheese, softened
- 2 tablespoons unsweetened instant tea
- 3/4 teaspoon ground cinnamon

COATING:
- 2 packages (3 ounces each) lemon gelatin
- 2 packages (3 ounces each) orange gelatin
- 2 packages (3 ounces each) strawberry gelatin
- 1/2 cup sugar

Mint leaves and additional apricot preserves

- In a large bowl, beat the eggs, sugar, oil, milk and vanilla until blended. Combine the flour and baking powder; gradually beat into the egg mixture.

- Roll into 3/4-in. balls. Place 2 in. apart on ungreased baking sheets; flatten slightly. Bake at 325° for 13-15 minutes or until firm. Remove to wire racks.

- While cookies are warm, use a sharp knife and small spoon to cut and scoop out about 1/2 teaspoon crumbs from the bottom of each cookie; set crumbs aside (about 1-1/2 cups) for filling. Cool cookies completely.

- In a small bowl, combine the filling ingredients; stir in reserved crumbs. Spoon into two cookies; spread a thin amount of filling on the cookie bottoms and press together to form a peach. Repeat with the remaining cookies and filling.

- In a shallow bowl, combine one package each of lemon and orange gelatin powder. Place one package of strawberry gelatin powder in another bowl. Place the sugar in a third bowl.

- Working with one cookie at a time, spritz cookie with water. Dip in lemon gelatin mixture, then in strawberry gelatin and then in sugar; spritz with additional water and add more gelatin as needed to create desired peach blush effect. Place on a wire rack to dry for 1 hour.

- Repeat with remaining cookies and packages of gelatin. Attach mint leaves to the top of each cookie with additional preserves. Store in the refrigerator.

YIELD: ABOUT 3-1/2 DOZEN.

hamburger cookies

PREP 30 min.

JULIE WELLINGTON • YOUNGSTOWN, OHIO

My husband loves peppermint patties, and our son is crazy for vanilla wafers. So I put the two together to make a creation that looks just like a burger. Kids of all ages get a kick out of these treats.

- 1/2 cup vanilla frosting

Red and yellow paste *or* gel food coloring
- 40 vanilla wafers
- 20 peppermint patties
- 1 teaspoon corn syrup
- 1 teaspoon sesame seeds

- Place 1/4 cup frosting in each of two small bowls. Tint one red and the other yellow. Frost the bottoms of 20 vanilla wafers yellow; top with a peppermint patty. Spread with red frosting. Brush tops of the remaining vanilla wafers with corn syrup; sprinkle with sesame seeds. Place over red frosting.

YIELD: ABOUT 1-1/2 DOZEN.

HAMBURGER COOKIES

christmas cookies

Savor the spirit of the season with this scrumptious assortment of homemade merry morsels. They're guaranteed to please!

PICTURED ABOVE: TINY TIM SANDWICH COOKIES, PAGE 83 • OATMEAL KISS COOKIES, PAGE 89
JELLY-TOPPED SUGAR COOKIES, PAGE 93 • CRANBERRY NUT COOKIES, PAGE 92

festive shortbread logs

PREP 30 min.
BAKE 10 min.

MICHELE FENNER • GIRARD, PENNSYLVANIA

I first made these rich and tender cookies as a teenager and now make them for my husband and our kids. The smiles on their faces are well worth the time and effort.

- 1 cup butter, softened
- 1/2 cup confectioners' sugar
- 1 teaspoon vanilla extract
- 2 cups all-purpose flour
- 1-1/2 cups semisweet chocolate chips
- 4 teaspoons shortening
- 3/4 cup ground walnuts

- In a large bowl, cream butter and confectioners' sugar until light and fluffy. Add vanilla. Gradually add flour and mix well.

- With lightly floured hands, shape tablespoonfuls into 2-in. logs. Place 2 in. apart on ungreased baking sheets. Bake at 350° for 9-11 minutes or until edges and bottom are lightly browned. Cool for 2-3 minutes before removing to wire racks.

- In a microwave, melt chocolate chips and shortening; stir until smooth. Drizzle chocolate over half of the cookies. Dip one end of remaining cookies into chocolate; allow excess to drip off. Sprinkle with walnuts. Place on waxed paper; let stand until set.

YIELD: 4 DOZEN.

PEPPERMINT MELTAWAYS

peppermint meltaways

PREP 30 min.
BAKE 10 min. + cooling

DENISE WHEELER • NEWAYGO, MICHIGAN

This recipe is very pretty and festive-looking on a dessert platter. I often cover a plate of these meltaways with red or green plastic wrap and a bright holiday bow in one corner. And yes, they really do melt in your mouth!

- 1 cup butter, softened
- 1/2 cup confectioners' sugar
- 1/2 teaspoon peppermint extract
- 1-1/4 cups all-purpose flour
- 1/2 cup cornstarch

FROSTING:

- 2 tablespoons butter, softened
- 1-1/2 cups confectioners' sugar
- 2 tablespoons 2% milk
- 1/4 teaspoon peppermint extract
- 2 to 3 drops red food coloring, optional
- 1/2 cup crushed peppermint candies

- In a small bowl, cream butter and confectioners' sugar until light and fluffy. Beat in extract. Combine flour and cornstarch; gradually add to creamed mixture and mix well.

- Shape into 1-in. balls. Place 2 in. apart on ungreased baking sheets. Bake at 350° for 10-12 minutes or until bottoms are lightly browned. Remove to wire racks to cool.

- In a small bowl, beat butter until fluffy. Add the confectioners' sugar, milk, extract and food coloring if desired; beat until smooth. Spread over the cooled cookies; sprinkle with crushed candies. Store in an airtight container.

YIELD: 3-1/2 DOZEN.

FESTIVE SHORTBREAD LOGS

snickerdoodles

PREP 15 min.
BAKE 10 min.

TASTE OF HOME TEST KITCHEN

The history of this whimsically named sweet treat is widely disputed, but the popularity of the classic cinnamon-sugar-coated cookie is undeniable!

- 1/2 cup butter, softened
- 1 cup plus 2 tablespoons sugar, *divided*
- 1 egg
- 1/2 teaspoon vanilla extract
- 1-1/2 cups all-purpose flour
- 1/4 teaspoon baking soda
- 1/4 teaspoon cream of tartar
- 1 teaspoon ground cinnamon

• In a large bowl, cream butter and 1 cup sugar until light and fluffy. Beat in the egg and vanilla. Combine the flour, baking soda and cream of tartar; gradually add to the creamed mixture and mix well. In a small bowl, combine the cinnamon and remaining sugar.

• Shape the dough into 1-in. balls; roll in the cinnamon-sugar. Place balls 2 in. apart onto ungreased baking sheets. Bake at 375° for 10-12 minutes or until lightly browned. Remove to wire racks to cool.

YIELD: 2-1/2 DOZEN.

SNICKERDOODLES

SITTIN' PRETTY PEANUT COOKIES

sittin' pretty peanut cookies

PREP 25 min. + chilling
BAKE 15 min.

GLORIA HURL • GALLOWAY, OHIO

For fun cookies that look as good as they taste, give my easy recipe a try. The delights have lots of peanut flavor, fluffy frosting and brightly colored peanut M&M's on top.

- 1/2 cup butter, softened
- 1/4 cup packed brown sugar
- 1 egg, *separated*
- 1/2 teaspoon vanilla extract
- 1 cup all-purpose flour
- 1/4 teaspoon salt
- 1 cup finely chopped peanuts, toasted
- 1/2 cup vanilla frosting
- Peanut M&M's

• In a bowl, cream butter and brown sugar. Beat in egg yolk and vanilla. Combine flour and salt; gradually add to creamed mixture. Cover and refrigerate for 2 hours.

• Roll into 1-in. balls. In a small bowl, beat egg white. Dip balls in egg white, then roll in the peanuts. Place the cookies 2 in. apart onto ungreased baking sheets.

• Bake at 350° for 5 minutes. Remove from the oven; using the end of a wooden spoon handle, make an indentation in the center of each cookie.

• Bake 7-9 minutes longer or until firm. Remove to wire racks to cool. Fill centers with vanilla frosting and top with M&M's.

YIELD: ABOUT 2 DOZEN.

toasted peanuts

Toasting peanuts intensifies their flavor and also gives them a pretty appearance, which can be especially desirable when you use them to top a baked item. Start by preheating the oven to 350°. Place the peanuts in a single layer on a shallow baking pan. Bake the peanuts for about 10 minutes, being sure to stir or shake them halfway through the baking time.

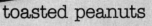

cranberry swirl biscotti

PREP 1 hour
BAKE 40 min. + cooling

LISA KILCUP ● GIG HARBOR, WASHINGTON

A friend of mine, who is known for her excellent dippers, shared this recipe with me. The mix of cranberries and cherry preserves is always so refreshing.

- 2/3 cup dried cranberries
- 1/2 cup cherry preserves
- 1/2 teaspoon ground cinnamon
- 1/2 cup butter, softened
- 2/3 cup sugar
- 2 eggs
- 1 teaspoon vanilla extract
- 2-1/4 cups all-purpose flour
- 3/4 teaspoon baking powder
- 1/4 teaspoon salt

GLAZE:

- 3/4 cup confectioners' sugar
- 1 tablespoon 2% milk
- 2 teaspoons butter, melted
- 1 teaspoon almond extract

● In a food processor, combine the cranberries, preserves and cinnamon. Cover and process until smooth; set aside.

● In a large bowl, cream butter and sugar until light and fluffy. Beat in eggs and vanilla. Combine the flour, baking powder and salt; gradually add to creamed mixture and mix well.

● Divide the dough in half. On a lightly floured surface, roll out each portion of dough into a 12-in. x 8-in. rectangle. Spread each with the cranberry filling; roll up jelly-roll style, starting with a short side.

● Place seam side down 4 in. apart on a lightly greased baking sheet. Bake at 325° for 25-30 minutes or until lightly browned.

● Carefully transfer logs to a cutting board; cool for 5 minutes. With a serrated knife, cut into 1/2-in. slices. Place 2 in. apart on lightly greased baking sheets. Bake 15 minutes longer or until centers are firm and dry. Remove to wire racks.

● In a small bowl, combine glaze ingredients; drizzle over warm biscotti. Cool completely. Store in an airtight container.

YIELD: ABOUT 2-1/2 DOZEN.

tiny tim sandwich cookies

PREP 45 min.
BAKE 10 min. + cooling

EUDORA DELEZENNE
PORT HURON, MICHIGAN

I have many special Christmas memories of my mother and I in the kitchen preparing these cute, bite-size sandwich cookies. You can vary the food coloring for holidays throughout the year.

- 1 cup sugar, *divided*
- 2 to 3 drops red food coloring
- 2 to 3 drops green food coloring
- 1/2 cup butter, softened
- 1/2 cup shortening
- 1/4 cup confectioners' sugar
- 1 teaspoon almond extract
- 2-1/3 cups all-purpose flour

FROSTING:

- 2 cups confectioners' sugar
- 3 tablespoons butter, softened
- 4-1/2 teaspoons heavy whipping cream
- 3/4 teaspoon almond extract
- Red and green food coloring, optional

● In a small bowl, combine 1/2 cup sugar and red food coloring; set aside. In another small bowl, combine remaining sugar with green food coloring; set aside.

● In a large bowl, cream the butter, shortening and confectioners' sugar until light and fluffy. Beat in extract. Gradually add flour and mix well. Shape into 1/2-in. balls.

● Place 1 in. apart on ungreased baking sheets. Coat the bottoms of two glasses with cooking spray, then dip one in red sugar and the other in green sugar. Flatten the cookies alternately with prepared glasses, redipping in the sugar as needed.

● Bake at 375° for 8-10 minutes or until edges are lightly browned. Remove to wire racks to cool completely.

● For the frosting, in a small bowl, combine the confectioners' sugar, butter, cream and extract. If desired, tint half of the frosting red and the other half green. Frost the bottoms of half of the cookies; top with the remaining cookies.

YIELD: 5 DOZEN.

TINY TIM SANDWICH COOKIES

red velvet cookies

PREP 30 min.
BAKE 15 min. + cooling

MINDY YOUNG • HANOVER, PENNSYLVANIA

These cake-like treats are a part of our holiday tradition. My mom made them when I was little, and now I bake them for my family.

- 1 cup shortening
- 1 cup sugar
- 3/4 cup packed brown sugar
- 3 eggs, *separated*
- 2 teaspoons red food coloring
- 4 cups all-purpose flour
- 3 tablespoons baking cocoa
- 3 teaspoons baking powder
- 1 teaspoon salt
- 1 cup buttermilk
- 2 cups (12 ounces) semisweet chocolate chips

FROSTING:

- 1-1/2 cups butter, softened
- 3-3/4 cups confectioners' sugar
- 1/8 teaspoon salt
- 3 to 4 tablespoons 2% milk

- In a large bowl, cream the shortening and sugars until light and fluffy. Beat in egg yolks and food coloring.
- Combine the flour, cocoa, baking powder and salt. Add the dry ingredients to the creamed mixture alternately with buttermilk, beating well after each addition.

- In another bowl with clean beaters, beat egg whites until stiff peaks form; fold into batter. Fold in chocolate chips.
- Drop dough by tablespoonfuls 2 in. apart onto greased baking sheets. Bake at 350° for 12-14 minutes or until set. Remove to wire racks to cool completely.
- In a large bowl, beat the butter, confectioners' sugar and salt until blended. Add enough milk to achieve desired consistency. Crumble eight cookies and set aside.
- Frost the remaining cookies; sprinkle with cookie crumbs. Store in an airtight container or freeze for up to 1 month.

YIELD: 7-1/2 DOZEN.

mexican wedding cakes

PREP 15 min.
BAKE 15 min.

SARITA JOHNSTON • SAN ANTONIO, TEXAS

It's a Mexican tradition to serve tender, shortbread-like cookies at weddings but we also enjoy them around the holidays. You can shape the dough into 2-in. crescents or 1-in. balls before baking.

- 2 cups butter, softened
- 1 cup confectioners' sugar
- 1 teaspoon vanilla extract
- 4 cups all-purpose flour
- 1 cup finely chopped pecans

Additional confectioners' sugar

- In a large bowl, cream butter and sugar until light and fluffy. Beat in vanilla. Gradually add flour and mix well. Stir in pecans.
- Shape tablespoonfuls into 2-in. crescents. Place 2 in. apart on ungreased baking sheets.
- Bake at 350° for 12-15 minutes or until lightly browned. Roll warm cookies in confectioners' sugar; cool on wire racks.

YIELD: ABOUT 6 DOZEN.

eggnog thumbprints

PREP 30 min. + chilling
BAKE 10 min. + cooling

MARY ANN LUDWIG • EDWARDSVILLE, ILLINOIS

These cute thumbprints always get recipe requests. They make special gifts and freeze well, too.

- 2/3 cup butter, softened
- 1/2 cup sugar
- 2 eggs, *separated*
- 1 teaspoon vanilla extract
- 1-1/2 cups all-purpose flour
- 1/4 teaspoon salt
- 1/8 teaspoon ground nutmeg
- 1 cup finely chopped walnuts

FILLING:

- 1/4 cup butter, softened
- 1 cup confectioners' sugar
- 1/4 teaspoon rum extract
- 1 to 2 teaspoons 2% milk
- 1 to 2 drops yellow food coloring, optional

- In a bowl, cream butter and sugar until light and fluffy. Beat in egg yolks and vanilla. Gradually stir in the flour, salt and nutmeg; mix well. Cover and refrigerate for 1 hour or until firm.
- In a small bowl, whisk egg whites until foamy. Shape dough into 1-in. balls; dip in egg whites, then roll in walnuts. Place 2 in. apart on baking sheets coated with cooking spray.
- Using a wooden spoon handle, make a 1/2-in. indentation in the center of each ball. Bake at 350° for 10-12 minutes or until center is set. Carefully remove from pans to wire racks to cool completely.
- For filling, combine the butter, confectioners' sugar, extract and enough milk to achieve a spreading consistency. Tint with food coloring if desired. Pipe about 1/2 teaspoon into each cookie.

YIELD: 4 DOZEN.

RED VELVET COOKIES

chewy coconut macaroons

PREP 10 min.
BAKE 20 min.

PEGGY KEY • GRANT, ALABAMA

These chewy cookies are my husband's favorites, so he requests them often. I like to make the macaroons on cold winter days and keep them in an airtight bowl on the kitchen counter. They never last long!

- 2-1/2 cups flaked coconut
- 3/4 cup all-purpose flour
- 1/8 teaspoon salt
- 1 can (14 ounces) fat-free sweetened condensed milk
- 1-1/2 teaspoons almond extract

• In a bowl, toss the coconut, flour and salt. Stir in milk and extract until blended (mixture will be thick and sticky).

• Drop by rounded teaspoonfuls 3 in. apart on lightly greased baking sheets. Bake at 300° for 18-22 minutes or just until golden brown. Cool for 2 minutes before removing from pans to wire racks.

YIELD: 2-1/2 DOZEN.

FLORENTINE COOKIE BARS

florentine cookie bars

PREP 1 hour + chilling
BAKE 20 min. + chilling

CAROLE SEPSTEAD • GRAFTON, WISCONSIN

Celebrate the season with these rich, chunky snacks. The whole family can join in the fun of decorating them.

- 1 cup butter, softened
- 2/3 cup sugar
- 1 egg
- 3 cups all-purpose flour

FILLING:

- 2 cups sugar
- 1-1/4 cups heavy whipping cream
- 3/4 cup butter, cubed
- 2/3 cup honey
- 4 cups sliced almonds
- 1-1/2 cups red *and/or* green candied cherries
- 3/4 cup dried currants

GARNISH:

- 1-1/4 pounds white candy coating, coarsely chopped

• In a large bowl, cream butter and sugar until light and fluffy. Beat in egg. Gradually add flour and mix well. Refrigerate for 30 minutes or until easy to handle.

• Roll dough into an ungreased 15-in. x 10-in. x 1-in. baking pan. Bake at 375° for 7-9 minutes or until lightly browned.

• Meanwhile, in a large heavy saucepan, combine the sugar, cream, butter and honey. Cook, stirring occasionally, until a candy thermometer reads 246° (firm-ball stage). Remove from the heat; stir in almonds, cherries and currants. Spread evenly into crust.

• Bake for 18-22 minutes or just until filling is set. Cool completely on a wire rack. Refrigerate overnight.

• Remove florentine from pan. With a sharp knife, trim edges of crust; discard the trim. Cut lengthwise into six strips; cut each strip into 16 triangles.

• In a microwave-safe bowl, melt candy coating; stir until smooth. Dip the short side of each triangle into candy coating; place on waxed paper. Drizzle with additional candy coating. Let stand until set. Cover and store in the refrigerator.

YIELD: 8 DOZEN.

EDITOR'S NOTE: We recommend that you test your candy thermometer before each use by bringing water to a boil; the thermometer should read 212°. Adjust your recipe temperature up or down based on your test.

CHEWY COCONUT MACAROONS

FESTIVE STARS

festive stars

PREP 50 min. + chilling
BAKE 10 min. + cooling

CAREN ZIMMERMAN • FRANKLIN, WISCONSIN

These clever interlocking cookies add delightful dimension to a holiday cookie assortment.

- 1/2 cup butter, softened
- 1/4 cup shortening
- 1 cup sugar
- 2 eggs
- 1 teaspoon vanilla extract
- 2-1/2 cups all-purpose flour
- 1 teaspoon baking powder
- 1/4 teaspoon salt
- 3/4 cup red colored sugar

- In a large bowl, cream the butter, shortening and sugar until light and fluffy. Beat in eggs and vanilla. Combine the flour, baking powder and salt; gradually add to creamed mixture and mix well. Chill for 1 hour or until easy to handle.

- On a lightly floured surface, roll out dough to 1/8-in. thickness. Cut with a floured 2-1/2-in. five-point star-shaped cookie cutter. Cut a vertical slit between two points on each star to just above the center; spread dough apart to form a 1/4-in. opening.

- Place 1 in. apart on ungreased baking sheets. Sprinkle with colored sugar. Bake at 400° for 6-7 minutes or until edges begin to brown. Remove to wire racks to cool. Assemble by placing two stars together at slits.

YIELD: ABOUT 3 DOZEN.

cherry chocolate nut cookies

PREP 30 min.
BAKE 10 min.

SYBIL NOBLE • HAMBURG, ARKANSAS

Each Christmas, I make about 600 cookies to share with family and friends. The holidays wouldn't be the same without several batches of these colorful goodies.

- 1/2 cup butter, softened
- 1/2 cup sugar
- 1/2 cup packed brown sugar
- 1 egg
- 1/4 cup 2% milk
- 1 teaspoon vanilla extract
- 2 cups all-purpose flour
- 1 teaspoon baking powder
- 1/2 teaspoon salt
- 1/4 teaspoon baking soda
- 1 cup (6 ounces) semisweet chocolate chips
- 3/4 cup chopped maraschino cherries
- 3/4 cup chopped pecans

- In a large bowl, cream butter and sugars until light and fluffy. Beat in the egg, milk and vanilla. Combine the flour, baking powder, salt and baking soda; gradually add to creamed mixture and mix well. Stir in remaining ingredients.

- Drop dough by tablespoonfuls 2 in. apart onto greased baking sheets. Bake at 375° for 10-12 minutes or until golden brown. Remove to wire racks to cool.

YIELD: 5 DOZEN.

homemade snow globes

PREP 1 hour + standing

GEORGIA KOHART • OAKWOOD, OHIO

You'll be snowed under with offers from little ones wanting to help put together these snow globes. Just make sure they don't nibble up all the ingredients before decorating!

- 2 cups confectioners' sugar
- 2 tablespoons plus 2 teaspoons water
- 4-1/2 teaspoons meringue powder
- 1/4 teaspoon cream of tartar
- 6 sugar cookies (about 3-1/2 inches)

Assorted decorations: miniature marshmallows, orange and brown jimmies, Fruit Roll-Ups, spearmint leaves, peppermint candies, edible glitter and holiday sprinkles

- 3 clear plastic ornaments (3 inches)

- In a small bowl, combine the confectioners' sugar, water, meringue powder and cream of tartar; beat on low speed just until combined. Beat on high for 4-5 minutes or until stiff peaks form. Cover frosting with a damp cloth between uses. If necessary, beat again on high speed to restore texture.

- Working with one cookie at a time, spread 2 tablespoons frosting over the top of cookie.

- For snowman, cut two miniature marshmallows in half. Attach three halves with a small amount of frosting. Decorate face with jimmies. For scarf, trim a thin 1-1/2-in. strip from a Fruit Roll-Up. Shape a toboggan from a strip of Fruit Roll-Up; attach toboggan to cookie. Attach snowman to toboggan. Add spearmint leaves for trees.

- With a dab of frosting, attach four peppermint candies to the bottom of each cookie. Let stand overnight to dry completely.

- To assemble, separate the ornaments into halves. Working with one cookie at a time, spread edge of ornament half with frosting. Place 1 teaspoon edible glitter and 1 teaspoon holiday sprinkles inside ornament; carefully invert decorated cookie onto ornament half, sealing edges. Use frosting and a star tip to pipe a decorative edge around globe. Let stand until set. Store in an airtight container.

YIELD: 6 SNOW GLOBES.

EDITOR'S NOTE: This recipe was tested with Crystal Keepsakes 80mm Everyday Ball-shaped Crystal Ornaments, available at craft stores. Meringue powder and edible glitter are available from Wilton Industries. Call 1-800/794-5866 or visit *www.wilton.com*.

tip

holiday cookies

To save time and still make a variety of cookies for holiday celebrations, get creative with a big batch of basic refrigerator sugar cookie dough. Slice some to make round cookies and top with colored sugar; roll some into balls and coat them with coconut or chopped nuts; and wrap the rest around fillings like dates, cherries and candies.

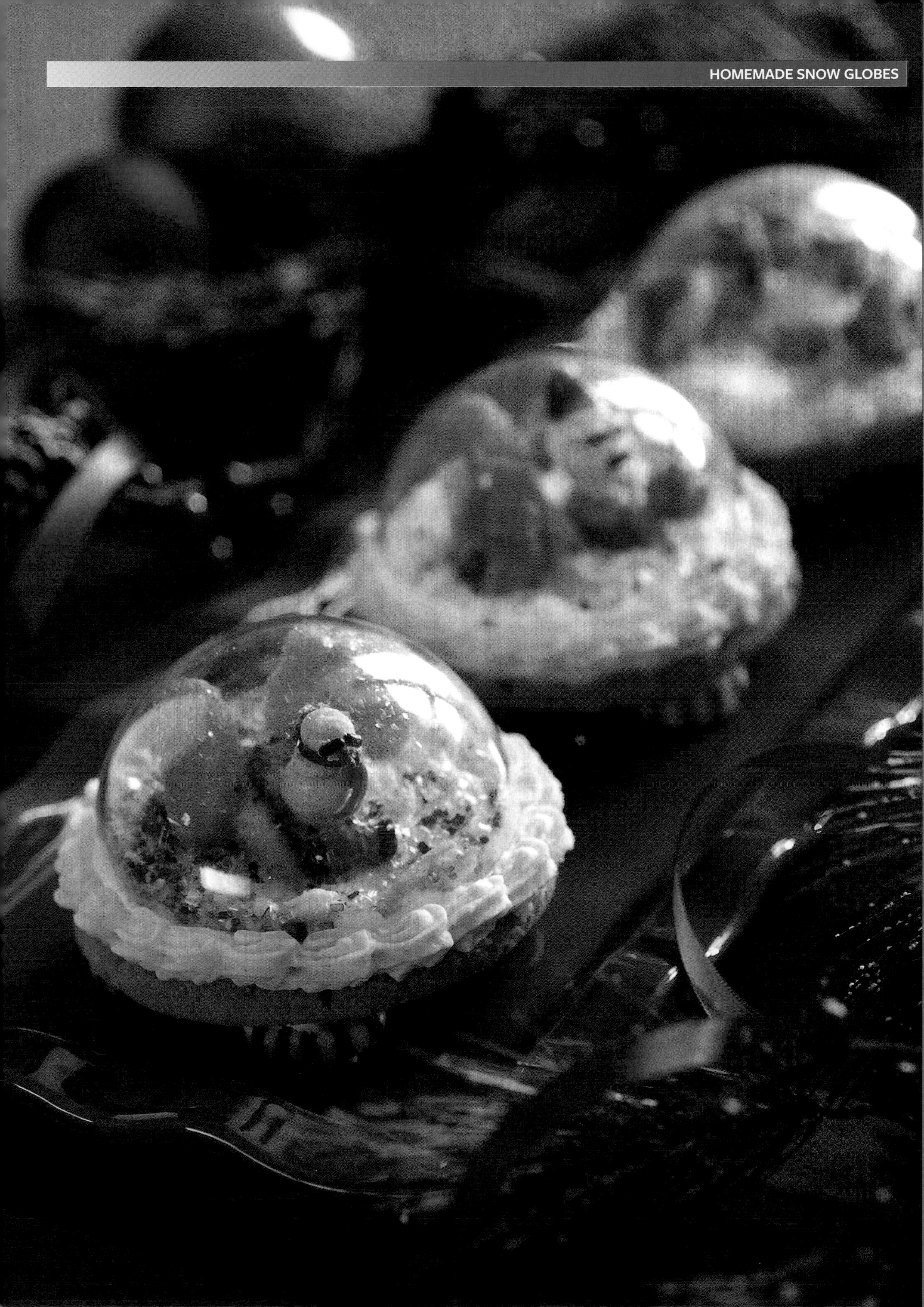

secret treat molasses cookies

PREP 30 min. + chilling
BAKE 10 min. + cooling

RUBY NEESE • LIBERTY, NORTH CAROLINA

This recipe has been passed down for generations. I've made the cookies for years, but like my mother, I only make them for special occasions. They're fun to decorate, and with a surprise flavor inside, delicious to eat.

- 1/2 cup butter, softened
- 1/2 cup packed brown sugar
- 1 egg
- 1/2 cup molasses
- 2-1/2 cups all-purpose flour
- 3/4 teaspoon baking soda
- 1/2 teaspoon salt
- 1/2 teaspoon ground cinnamon
- 1/2 teaspoon ground ginger
- 1/2 cup strawberry preserves

GLAZE:
- 1-2/3 cups confectioners' sugar
- 2 tablespoons water
- 1/4 teaspoon vanilla extract

• In a large bowl, cream butter and brown sugar until light and fluffy. Beat in egg and molasses. Combine the flour, baking soda, salt, cinnamon and ginger; gradually add to creamed mixture and mix well. (The dough will be very stiff.) Cover and refrigerate for 1-2 hours or until easy to handle.

• On a lightly floured surface, roll dough to 1/8-in. thickness; cut into 2-1/4-in. to 2-1/2-in. circles. Place 1/2 teaspoon preserves on half of the circles; top with remaining circles. Pinch edges together to seal. Place on greased baking sheets.

• Bake at 350° for 10 minutes or until lightly browned. Cool on wire racks. Combine glaze ingredients and frost cooled cookies.

YIELD: ABOUT 2 DOZEN.

cranberry pecan sandies

PREP 20 min.
BAKE 15 min.

TERESA JARRELL • DANVILLE, WEST VIRGINIA

You will love the recipe for my delightful, delicate, crisp cookies featuring pecans, cranberries and a hint of orange. They're delectable.

- 1 package (15.6 ounces) cranberry-orange quick bread mix
- 1/2 cup butter, melted
- 1 egg
- 2 tablespoons orange juice
- 3/4 cup chopped pecans
- 30 to 36 pecan halves

ORANGE GLAZE:
- 1 cup confectioners' sugar
- 3 to 4 teaspoons orange juice

• In a large bowl, combine the bread mix, butter, egg and orange juice. Stir in chopped pecans. Roll into 1-in. balls. Place 2 in. apart on ungreased baking sheets. Flatten with the bottom of a glass coated with cooking spray. Press a pecan half into center of each cookie.

• Bake cookies at 350° for 12-14 minutes or until lightly browned. Cool for 1 minute before removing to wire racks. In a small bowl, whisk glaze ingredients. Drizzle over cookies.

YIELD: 2-1/2 TO 3 DOZEN.

cherry-almond balls

PREP 15 min.
BAKE 15 min. + cooling

ADA ROST • HERNANDO, FLORIDA

I have included this treat in my Christmas baking for years, much to the enjoyment of my family. Instead of almonds, I'll sometimes use pecans, and everyone seems to like those as well.

- 3/4 cup butter, softened
- 1/3 cup confectioners' sugar
- 1 teaspoon vanilla extract
- 2 cups all-purpose flour
- 1/4 teaspoon salt
- 1/2 cup chopped almonds
- 60 red *and/or* green candied cherries

Additional confectioners' sugar

• In a small bowl, cream butter and sugar until light and fluffy. Add vanilla. Combine flour and salt; gradually add to creamed mixture and mix well. Stir in almonds.

• Roll 1 teaspoon of dough around each cherry. Place on greased baking sheets. Bake at 325° for 15-20 minutes or until lightly browned. Remove to wire racks to cool slightly; roll in confectioners' sugar.

YIELD: 5 DOZEN.

SECRET TREAT MOLASSES COOKIES

OATMEAL KISS COOKIES

- Place 2 in. apart on parchment paper-lined baking sheets. Bake at 350° for 10-12 minutes or until edges are golden brown. Remove to wire racks.

YIELD: 2 DOZEN.

orange dreams

PREP 10 min.
BAKE 10 min. + cooling

SUSAN WARREN
NORTH MANCHESTER, INDIANA

A fellow teacher shared this recipe with me. We have several great cooks on our teaching staff, and each of us takes turns bringing special goodies to the lounge. These moist, chewy cookies with a pleasant orange flavor are a favorite.

1	cup butter, softened
1/2	cup sugar
1/2	cup packed brown sugar
1	egg
1	tablespoon grated orange peel
2-1/4	cups all-purpose flour
3/4	teaspoon baking soda
1/2	teaspoon salt
1-1/2	cups white baking chips

- In a large bowl, cream butter and sugars until light and fluffy. Beat in egg and orange peel. Combine the flour, baking soda and salt; gradually add to the creamed mixture and mix well. Stir in baking chips.

- Drop by rounded tablespoonfuls 2 in. apart onto ungreased baking sheets. Bake at 350° for 10-12 minutes or until golden brown. Remove to wire racks to cool.

YIELD: 4-1/2 DOZEN.

ORANGE DREAMS

oatmeal
kiss cookies

PREP 35 min.
BAKE 10 min.

ANNA MARY KNIER • MOUNT JOY, PENNSYLVANIA

This is a nice change from usual peanut butter kisses served on holiday cookie trays. Kids can join in the fun of making these mouthwatering morsels by simply unwrapping the kisses.

1/2	cup butter, softened
1/2	cup shortening
1	cup sugar
1	cup packed brown sugar
2	eggs
2	cups all-purpose flour
1	teaspoon baking soda
1	teaspoon salt
2-1/4	cups quick-cooking oats
1	cup chopped nuts
72	milk chocolate kisses

- In a large bowl, cream the butter, shortening and sugars until light and fluffy. Add eggs, one at a time, beating well after each addition. Combine the flour, baking soda and salt; gradually add to creamed mixture and mix well. Stir in oats and nuts. Roll into 1-in. balls. Place 2 in. apart on ungreased baking sheets.

- Bake at 375° for 10-12 minutes or until lightly browned. Immediately press a chocolate kiss in the center of each cookie. Remove to wire racks to cool.

YIELD: 6 DOZEN.

colorful candy
bar cookies

PREP 35 min.
BAKE 10 min.

TASTE OF HOME TEST KITCHEN

No one will ever guess these sweet snacks with the candy bar center start with store-bought dough. Roll them in colored sugar or just dip the tops for even faster assembly. If you don't have miniature candy bars on hand, you can slice regular size Snickers candy bars into 1-inch pieces.

1/2	tube refrigerated sugar cookie dough, softened
1/4	cup all-purpose flour
24	miniature Snickers candy bars

Red and green colored sugar

- In a small bowl, beat cookie dough and flour until combined. Shape 1-1/2 teaspoonfuls of dough around each candy bar. Roll dough in colored sugar.

chocolate-covered cherry cookies

PREP 45 min. + chilling
BAKE 15 min. + cooling

VERONICA STRANGE
GLOCESTER, RHODE ISLAND

I first tasted these delights at a cookie swap. Now I like to make them every Christmas. Folks who haven't had them are surprised by the hidden treasure inside.

- 24 maraschino cherries
- 1/2 cup butter, softened
- 3/4 cup packed brown sugar
- 1 tablespoon maraschino cherry juice
- 1 teaspoon vanilla extract
- 1-1/2 cups all-purpose flour
- 1/8 teaspoon salt
- 1 cup milk chocolate chips, *divided*
- 1/2 teaspoon shortening

- Pat cherries with paper towels to remove excess moisture; set aside. In a large bowl, cream butter and brown sugar until light and fluffy. Beat in cherry juice and vanilla. Combine flour and salt; gradually add to creamed mixture and mix well. Cover and refrigerate for 1 hour or until dough is easy to handle.

- Insert a chocolate chip into each maraschino cherry. Wrap a tablespoon of dough around each cherry. Place 1 in. apart on ungreased baking sheets.

- Bake at 350° for 15-17 minutes or until set and edges are lightly browned. Remove to wire racks to cool.

- In a microwave, melt remaining chips and shortening; stir until smooth. Dip tops of cookies in melted chocolate; allow excess to drip off. Place on wax paper; let stand until set. Store in an airtight container.

YIELD: 2 DOZEN.

CHOCOLATE-COVERED CHERRY COOKIES

raspberry chocolate rugalach

PREP 40 min. + chilling
BAKE 20 min. + cooling

G.P. BUSAROW • WHITEHALL, MONTANA

Since we celebrate both Hanukkah and Christmas, these cookies are always on the menu. They can be covered and refrigerated overnight or frozen for up to two months.

- 1/2 cup butter, softened
- 4 ounces cream cheese, softened
- 1 cup all-purpose flour
- 1/4 teaspoon salt

FILLING:

- 1/4 cup dried currants
- 2 tablespoons sugar
- 1/2 teaspoon ground cinnamon
- 1/4 cup seedless raspberry jam
- 2/3 cup finely chopped pecans

- 1/4 cup miniature semisweet chocolate chips

- In a large bowl, beat butter and cream cheese until smooth. Combine flour and salt; gradually add to creamed mixture and mix well.

- Divide the dough in half; form into two balls. Flatten to 5-in. circles; wrap in plastic wrap. Refrigerate for 8 hours or overnight.

- Place currants in a small bowl. Cover with boiling water; let stand for 5 minutes. Drain well and set aside. Combine sugar and cinnamon; set aside.

- On a lightly floured surface or pastry mat, roll one portion of dough into an 11-in. circle. Brush with half of the jam. Sprinkle with half of the cinnamon-sugar, pecans, chocolate chips and currants; press down gently.

- Cut into 16 wedges. Roll up wedges from the wide end and place point side down 2 in. apart on a parchment paper-lined baking sheet. Curve ends to form a crescent. Cover and refrigerate for 30 minutes before baking. Repeat with remaining dough and filling.

- Bake at 350° for 18-22 minutes or until golden brown. Remove to wire racks to cool.

YIELD: ABOUT 2-1/2 DOZEN.

rugalach

Rugalach (ruhg-uh-lukh) is a traditional Jewish cookie normally prepared for Hanukkah. The dough for these bite-size, crescent-shaped cookies is prepared with cream cheese, which results in a dense texture and rich flavor. Rugalach can be made with a variety of fillings, including fruit, raisins, nuts, jam and poppy seeds.

cherry bonbon cookies

PREP 20 min.
BAKE 15 min. + cooling

LORI DANIELS • BEVERLY, WEST VIRGINIA

These goodies have always been part of my Christmas cookie baking. It is sure to be a favorite in your home, too.

 36 maraschino cherries
  1 cup butter, softened
1-1/2 cups confectioners' sugar
  1 tablespoon 2% milk
  3 teaspoons vanilla extract
2-3/4 cups all-purpose flour
 1/4 teaspoon salt

CHRISTMAS GLAZE:

1-1/4 cups confectioners' sugar
  1 to 2 tablespoons water
Red and green liquid food coloring
Colored sprinkles

CHOCOLATE GLAZE:

  1 cup confectioners' sugar
  1 to 2 tablespoons water
  1 ounce unsweetened chocolate, melted
  1 teaspoon vanilla extract
 1/2 cup chopped pecans *or* walnuts

• Pat cherries dry with paper towels; set aside. In a large bowl, cream butter and confectioners' sugar until light and fluffy. Beat in milk and vanilla. Combine flour and salt; gradually add to creamed mixture.

• Shape one tablespoonful of dough around each cherry, forming a ball. Place 2 in. apart on ungreased baking sheets. Bake at 350° for 14-16 minutes or until bottoms are browned. Remove to wire racks to cool.

• For Christmas glaze, in a small bowl, combine confectioners' sugar and enough water to achieve a dipping consistency. Transfer half of the glaze to another bowl; tint one bowl red and the other green. Dip the tops of nine cookies in red glaze and nine cookies in green glaze, then decorate with sprinkles. Let stand until set.

• For chocolate glaze, in a small bowl, combine confectioners' sugar and enough water to achieve dipping consistency. Stir in chocolate and vanilla. Dip the tops of remaining cookies in glaze, then sprinkle with nuts. Let stand until set.

YIELD: 3 DOZEN.

BUTTERY BOW COOKIES

buttery bow cookies

PREP 1 hour + chilling
BAKE 10 min.

DIANA MANGELSEN • FREDERIC, WISCONSIN

My aunt shared this recipe with me many years ago. Family and friends look for these tasty edible bows on my cookie trays each and every Christmas.

  3 cups all-purpose flour
  1 cup confectioners' sugar
  1 teaspoon baking powder
 1/4 teaspoon salt
  1 cup cold butter, cubed
  1 egg, lightly beaten
 1/2 cup heavy whipping cream
  3 tablespoons butter, melted
Red and green colored sugar

• In a large bowl, combine the flour, sugar, baking powder and salt; cut in butter until crumbly. Combine egg and cream; gradually beat into crumb mixture until a ball forms. Cover and refrigerate for 30 minutes or until easy to handle.

• Divide the dough into three portions. On a lightly floured surface, roll each portion into an 8-in. x 6-in. rectangle. Brush with melted butter; sprinkle with colored sugar. Cut into 8-in.-long x 1/4-in.-wide strips. Place 2 in. apart on ungreased baking sheets; form into bows.

• Bake at 350° for 10-12 minutes or until bottoms are lightly browned. Cool for 1 minute before carefully removing from pans to wire racks to cool completely.

YIELD: 6 DOZEN.

CHERRY BONBON COOKIES

CHOCOLATE CHIP BISCOTTI

chocolate chip biscotti

PREP 30 min.
BAKE 40 min. + cooling

THERESA SMITH • LEE, NEW HAMPSHIRE

With a hint of apricot flavor, these chocolate chip biscotti taste great alongside a hot cup of coffee or tea. My guests are always happy to receive a batch as a gift every Christmas from me.

- 3/4 cup butter, softened
- 1-1/2 cups plus 1-1/2 teaspoons sugar, *divided*
- 4 eggs
- 3 teaspoons vanilla extract
- 4 cups all-purpose flour
- 3 teaspoons baking powder
- 1/2 teaspoon salt
- 1 cup finely chopped dried apricots
- 1 cup swirled semisweet and white chocolate chips

- In a large bowl, cream butter and 1-1/2 cups sugar. Add the eggs, one at a time, beating well after each addition. Beat in vanilla.

- Combine the flour, baking powder and salt; gradually add to creamed mixture. Stir in apricots and chocolate chips.

- Divide dough in half. On ungreased baking sheets, shape each portion into a 12-in. x 2-1/2-in. rectangle. Sprinkle with remaining sugar. Bake at 325° for 30 minutes or until firm. Cool for 5 minutes.

- Transfer to a cutting board; cut diagonally with a serrated knife into 1/2-in. slices. Place cut side down on ungreased baking sheets. Bake for 6-8 minutes or until golden brown.

- Remove to wire racks to cool. Store in an airtight container.

YIELD: 3 DOZEN.

cranberry nut cookies

PREP 15 min.
BAKE 20 min.

MACHELLE WALL • ROSAMOND, CALIFORNIA

In the fall, I stock up on fresh cranberries and freeze them so I can make these tangy, buttery goodies throughout the year.

- 2/3 cup butter, softened
- 1 cup sugar
- 1 cup packed brown sugar
- 1 egg
- 1/4 cup 2% milk
- 2 tablespoons lemon juice
- 3 cups all-purpose flour
- 1/4 cup ground walnuts
- 1 teaspoon baking powder
- 1/2 teaspoon salt
- 1/4 teaspoon baking soda
- 2-1/2 cups halved fresh *or* frozen cranberries
- 1 cup chopped walnuts

- In a large bowl, cream butter and sugars until light and fluffy. Beat in the egg, milk and lemon juice. Combine the flour, ground walnuts, baking powder, salt and baking soda; gradually add to the creamed mixture and mix well. Stir in the cranberries and chopped walnuts.

- Drop by heaping tablespoonfuls 2 in. apart onto lightly greased baking sheets. Bake at 350° for 16-18 minutes or until golden brown. Remove to wire racks to cool.

YIELD: 5 DOZEN.

hedgehog cookies

PREP 10 min.
BAKE 12 min.

SANDRA PICHON • MEMPHIS, TENNESSEE

These little snacks are as cute as can be and delicious, too. A lady from my garden club shared this recipe one Christmas, but they're perfect for any occasion. They're a hit with both kids and grown-ups.

- 1 cup finely chopped walnuts
- 1/2 cup finely chopped dates
- 1/2 cup packed brown sugar
- 1 cup flaked coconut, *divided*
- 1 egg

- In a bowl, combine the walnuts, dates and brown sugar. Add 1/2 cup coconut and the egg; mix well. Shape into 1-in. balls; roll in remaining coconut. Place on greased baking sheets.

- Bake at 350° for 12-13 minutes or until lightly browned. Remove to wire racks to cool.

YIELD: ABOUT 1-1/2 DOZEN.

CRANBERRY NUT COOKIES

JELLY-TOPPED SUGAR COOKIES

- In a small bowl, beat eggs and sugar; stir in milk and vanilla. Combine flour and salt; gradually add to batter until smooth.

- Heat 2-1/2 in. of oil to 375° in a deep-fat fryer or electric skillet. Place rosette iron in hot oil, then dip in batter, three-fourths up the sides of iron (do not let batter run over top of iron). Immediately place in hot oil; loosen rosette with fork and remove iron.

- Fry rosettes 1-2 minutes on each side or until golden brown. Remove to paper towel-lined wire racks. Repeat with remaining batter.

- For icing, combine the confectioners' sugar, vanilla and enough water to achieve a dipping consistency. Dip edges of rosettes into icing; let dry on wire racks.

YIELD: ABOUT 5 DOZEN.

poppy seed thumbprints

PREP 15 min.

BAKE 10 min. + cooling

KELLY PEMBER • WHEELER, WISCONSIN

These crisp little thumbprints have the fantastic flavor of shortbread. A tiny dollop of raspberry preserves on top makes them colorful and festive for holiday celebrations.

- 1/2 cup butter, softened
- 1 cup confectioners' sugar
- 1/2 cup canola oil
- 1 egg
- 1 teaspoon vanilla extract
- 2-2/3 cups all-purpose flour
- 1/2 teaspoon salt
- 2 tablespoons poppy seeds
- 1 teaspoon grated lemon peel
- 1/3 cup seedless raspberry preserves

- In a large bowl, cream butter and confectioners' sugar until light and fluffy. Beat in the oil, egg and vanilla.

- Combine the flour and salt; gradually add to creamed mixture and mix well. Beat in poppy seeds and lemon peel.

- Shape into 1-in. balls. Place 1 in. apart onto ungreased baking sheets. Using a wooden spoon handle, make an indentation in the center of each cookie. Spoon 1/4 teaspoon preserves into each cookie.

- Bake at 325° for 10-12 minutes or until bottoms are lightly browned. Remove to wire racks to cool.

YIELD: 5 DOZEN.

jelly-topped sugar cookies

PREP 20 min.

BAKE 10 min.

JUNE QUINN • KALAMAZOO, MICHIGAN

I love this fast-to-fix drop sugar cookie. Top each one with your favorite flavor of jam or jelly.

- 3/4 cup sugar
- 3/4 cup canola oil
- 2 eggs
- 2 teaspoons vanilla extract
- 1 teaspoon lemon extract
- 1 teaspoon grated lemon peel
- 2 cups all-purpose flour
- 2 teaspoons baking powder
- 1/2 teaspoon salt
- 1/2 cup jam *or* jelly

- In a large bowl, beat the sugar and oil until blended. Beat in eggs, extracts and lemon peel. Combine the flour, baking powder and salt; gradually add to sugar mixture and mix well.

- Drop by rounded tablespoonfuls 2 in. apart onto ungreased baking sheets. Coat bottom of a glass with cooking spray, then dip glass in sugar. Flatten cookies with prepared glass, redipping in sugar as needed.

- Place 1/4 teaspoon jam or jelly in the center of each cookie. Bake at 400° for 8-10 minutes or until set. Remove to wire racks to cool.

YIELD: ABOUT 3-1/2 DOZEN.

rosettes

PREP 20 min.

COOK 30 min.

IOLA EGLE • BELLA VISTA, ARKANSAS

Dipping the edges of these traditional favorites in icing defines their lacy pattern.

- 2 eggs
- 2 teaspoons sugar
- 1 cup 2% milk
- 3 teaspoons vanilla extract
- 1 cup all-purpose flour
- 1/4 teaspoon salt

Oil for deep-fat frying

ICING:

- 2 cups confectioners' sugar
- 1 teaspoon vanilla extract
- 1 to 3 tablespoons water

brownies & bars

There's no better (or easier) way to satisfy your sweet tooth than with a brownie or bar. Indulge your fancy with these yummy sensations.

PICTURED ABOVE: CHOCOLATE NUT BARS, PAGE 96 • CARAMEL CANDY BARS, PAGE 98
RASPBERRY PATCH CRUMB BARS, PAGE 105 • PEANUT BUTTER BROWNIES, PAGE 101

LEMON COCONUT SQUARES

dark chocolate orange blondies

PREP 20 min.
BAKE 20 min. + cooling

KERRI PELZ
HENDERSONVILLE, NORTH CAROLINA

This blondie is a nice change from the traditional one, especially for those who crave the combo of orange and chocolate. An 8-inch loaf pan makes the perfect amount for two to snack on!

- 2 tablespoons butter, softened
- 1/2 cup packed brown sugar
- 2 tablespoons beaten egg
- 1/2 teaspoon grated orange peel
- 1/4 teaspoon almond extract
- 1/4 teaspoon orange extract
- 1/2 cup all-purpose flour
- 1/4 teaspoon baking powder
- 1/4 teaspoon salt
- 1/8 teaspoon baking soda
- 1/3 cup dark chocolate chips
- 1/4 cup chopped walnuts, optional

- In a small bowl, cream butter and brown sugar until light and fluffy. Beat in the egg, orange peel and extracts.

- Combine the flour, baking powder, salt and baking soda; gradually add to the creamed mixture. Stir in the chocolate chips and walnuts if desired.

- Spread into an 8-in. x 4-in. loaf pan coated with cooking spray. Bake at 350° for 20-25 minutes or until a toothpick inserted near the center comes out clean. Cool on a wire rack.

YIELD: 6 SERVINGS.

DARK CHOCOLATE ORANGE BLONDIES

lemon coconut squares

PREP 15 min.
BAKE 35 min.

DONNA BIDDLE • ELMIRA, NEW YORK

The tangy lemon flavor of this no-fuss dessert is especially delicious on a warm day. It reminds me of selling lemonade on the sidewalk as a little girl.

- 1-1/2 cups all-purpose flour
- 1/2 cup confectioners' sugar
- 3/4 cup cold butter
- 4 eggs
- 1-1/2 cups sugar
- 1/2 cup lemon juice
- 1 teaspoon baking powder
- 3/4 cup flaked coconut

- In a small bowl, combine flour and confectioners' sugar; cut in the butter until crumbly. Press into a lightly greased 13-in. x 9-in. baking dish. Bake at 350° for 15 minutes.

- Meanwhile, in another small bowl, beat the eggs, sugar, lemon juice and baking powder until combined. Pour over crust; sprinkle with the coconut.

- Bake at 350° for 20-25 minutes or until bars are golden brown. Cool on a wire rack. Cut into squares.

YIELD: 48 SERVINGS.

crunchy peanut bars

PREP 20 min. + chilling

NOLA BURSKI • LAKEVILLE, MINNESOTA

You will only need a handful of ingredients to fix these no-bake bars, which are packed with peanut flavor. The recipe makes a small pan, so you won't be tempted with lots of leftovers!

- 1/4 cup light corn syrup
- 2 tablespoons brown sugar
- 1 tablespoon sugar
- 1/4 cup creamy peanut butter
- 1-1/2 cups cornflakes
- 1/4 cup Spanish peanuts
- 1/2 cup milk chocolate chips, melted

- In a large saucepan over medium heat, bring corn syrup and sugars to a boil. Remove from the heat; stir in peanut butter. Fold in cornflakes and peanuts.

- Gently press into a 9-in. x 5-in. loaf pan coated with cooking spray. Spread melted chocolate evenly over top. Cover and refrigerate for 1 hour or until firm. Cut into bars.

YIELD: 8 SERVINGS.

CHOCOLATE NUT BARS

chocolate nut bars

PREP 30 min.

BAKE 15 min. + cooling

LISA DARLING • ROCHESTER, NEW YORK

When I ask my husband what he would like me to bake, he often asks for these fudgy, nutty bars. They are definitely his favorite!

- 1 cup butter, softened
- 2 cups all-purpose flour
- 1/2 cup sugar
- 1/4 teaspoon salt
- 1 can (14 ounces) sweetened condensed milk
- 2 cups (12 ounces) semisweet chocolate chips, *divided*
- 1 teaspoon vanilla extract
- 1/2 cup chopped macadamia nuts
- 1/2 cup chopped walnuts
- 1/2 cup chopped pecans
- 1/2 cup milk chocolate chips

- In a large bowl, beat butter until fluffy. Add the flour, sugar and salt; beat just until crumbly. Set aside 1 cup for topping. Press remaining crumb mixture into a greased 13-in. x 9-in. baking pan. Bake at 350° for 10-12 minutes or until set and edges begin to brown.

- Meanwhile, in a small saucepan, combine milk and 1-1/2 cups semisweet chocolate chips. Cook and stir until chips are melted. Remove from the heat; stir in vanilla. Spread mixture over crust.

- Combine the nuts and milk chocolate chips with the remaining 1/2 cup of semisweet chocolate chips and crumb mixture. Sprinkle over filling. Bake for 15-20 minutes or until center is set. Cool on a wire rack. Cut into bars.

YIELD: 36 SERVINGS.

banana nut brownies

PREP: 10 min.

BAKE: 40 min. + cooling

CHRISTINE MOL • GRAND RAPIDS, MICHIGAN

This treasured recipe comes from my grandmother. Anytime there are ripe bananas around our house, we know it's time to make a batch of these sweet, chocolaty treats.

- 1/2 cup butter, melted, cooled
- 1 cup sugar
- 3 tablespoons baking cocoa
- 2 eggs, lightly beaten
- 1 tablespoon milk
- 1 teaspoon vanilla extract
- 1/2 cup all-purpose flour
- 1 teaspoon baking powder
- 1/4 teaspoon salt
- 1 cup mashed ripe bananas (2-1/2 to 3 medium)
- 1/2 cup chopped walnuts

Confectioners' sugar, optional

- In a bowl, combine butter, sugar and cocoa. Stir in eggs, milk and vanilla. Blend in flour, baking powder and salt. Stir in the bananas and nuts.

- Pour batter into a greased 9-in. square baking pan. Bake at 350° for 40-45 minutes or until brownies test done. Cool on a wire rack. Just before serving, dust with confectioners' sugar if desired.

YIELD: 16 SERVINGS.

tiramisu brownies

PREP 25 min.

BAKE 45 min. + cooling

ANNA-MARIA CARPANZANO • WHITBY, ONTARIO

Tiramisu and brownies—what a great combination! This easy recipe gives you the traditional tiramisu flavor you adore minus the fuss.

- 12 ounces semisweet chocolate, chopped
- 1 cup butter, softened
- 1-1/3 cups plus 1/4 cup sugar, *divided*
- 8 eggs
- 1 cup cake flour
- 1/4 cup instant coffee granules *or* espresso powder
- 2 cartons (8 ounces *each*) Mascarpone cheese
- 2 teaspoons vanilla extract
- 1 teaspoon baking cocoa

- In a large microwave-safe bowl, melt the chocolate. Stir until smooth; cool slightly. Beat in the butter. Gradually beat in 1-1/3 cups sugar. Add six eggs, one at a time, beating well after each addition.

- Combine flour and coffee granules; add to chocolate mixture. Beat on low speed just until combined; set aside.

- For filling, in a small bowl, beat the cheese, vanilla, remaining sugar and remaining eggs until smooth.

- Pour 4 cups of the chocolate batter into a greased 13-in. x 9-in. baking pan. Spread with filling. Top with remaining batter, spreading evenly to completely cover filling.

- Bake at 350° for 45-50 minutes or until the center is almost set and brownies begin to pull away from sides of pan.

- Cool on a wire rack. Dust with cocoa. Cut into squares. Store in the refrigerator.

YIELD: 36 SERVINGS.

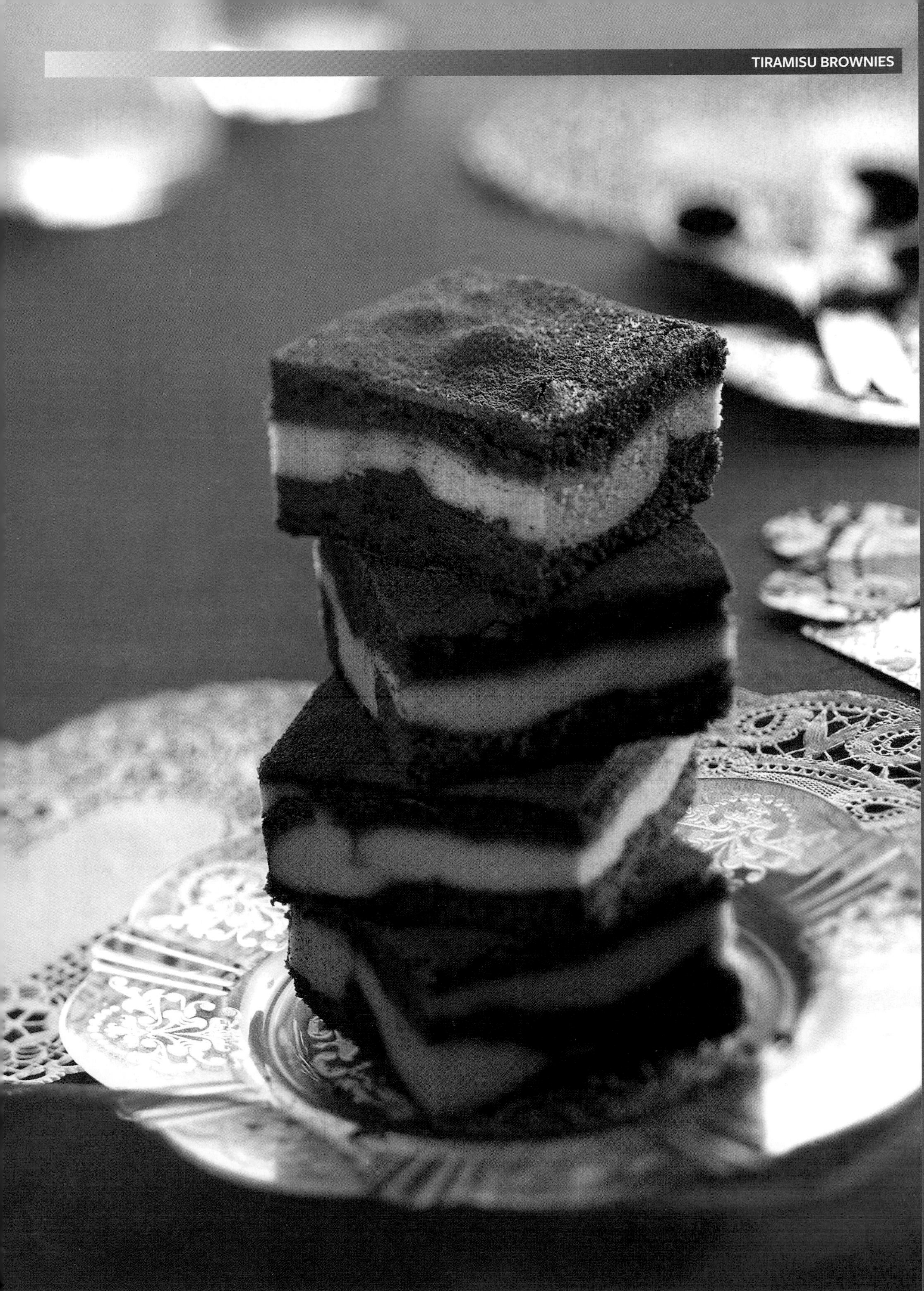

MACADAMIA NUT BROWNIES

macadamia nut brownies

PREP 10 min.
BAKE 20 min.

VALERIE MITCHELL • OLATHE, KANSAS

Craving chocolate? Take a big bite into one of these chewy, cake-like brownies. The macadamia nuts add a pleasant crunch.

- 3 tablespoons butter
- 1 ounce unsweetened chocolate
- 1 egg
- 2/3 cup sugar
- 1/2 teaspoon instant coffee granules
- 1/2 teaspoon vanilla extract
- 1/3 cup all-purpose flour
- 1/4 teaspoon baking powder
- 1/4 cup chopped macadamia nuts

- In a microwave-safe bowl, melt butter and chocolate; stir until smooth. Cool slightly.

- In a small bowl, beat the egg, sugar and coffee granules. Stir in vanilla and chocolate mixture. Combine flour and baking powder; gradually add to chocolate mixture.

- Spread into a 9-in. x 5-in. loaf pan coated with cooking spray. Sprinkle with nuts. Bake at 350° for 20-25 minutes or until brownies begin to pull away from sides of pan. Cool on a wire rack.

YIELD: 6 SERVINGS.

caramel candy bars

PREP 20 min.
BAKE 15 min. + chilling

JEANNIE KLUGH • LANCASTER, PENNSYLVANIA

You'll love these delicious, buttery bars. They're so rich that a small portion may be enough to satisfy your sweet tooth.

- 1/2 cup butter, softened
- 1/2 cup packed brown sugar
- 1-1/3 cups all-purpose flour

CARAMEL LAYER:
- 1 package (14 ounces) caramels
- 1/3 cup butter, cubed
- 1/3 cup evaporated milk
- 1-2/3 cups confectioners' sugar
- 1 cup chopped pecans

CHOCOLATE DRIZZLE:
- 1/4 cup semisweet chocolate chips
- 1 teaspoon shortening

- In a large bowl, cream butter and brown sugar until light and fluffy. Beat in flour until blended. Press into a greased 13-in. x 9-in. baking dish. Bake at 350° for 12-15 minutes or until golden brown.

- In a small saucepan over medium-low heat, melt the caramels and butter with milk until smooth, stirring occasionally. Remove from the heat; stir in confectioners' sugar and pecans. Spread over crust.

- In a microwave, melt chocolate chips and shortening; stir until smooth. Drizzle over caramel layer. Cover and refrigerate for 2 hours or until firm. Cut into bars.

YIELD: 24 SERVINGS.

cookie dough brownies

PREP 20 min. + chilling
BAKE 30 min. + cooling

WENDY BAILEY • ELIDA, OHIO

When I take these rich brownies to any get-together, I carry the recipe, too, because it always gets requested. Children of all ages love the tempting "cookie dough" filling. This special treat is typically the first to be gone from the buffet table—even before the entrees!

- 4 eggs
- 1 cup canola oil
- 2 cups sugar
- 2 teaspoons vanilla extract
- 1-1/2 cups all-purpose flour
- 1/2 cup baking cocoa
- 1/2 teaspoon salt

CARAMEL CANDY BARS

1/2 cup chopped walnuts, optional

FILLING:

1/2 cup butter, softened

1/2 cup packed brown sugar

1/4 cup sugar

2 tablespoons 2% milk

1 teaspoon vanilla extract

1 cup all-purpose flour

GLAZE:

1 cup (6 ounces) semisweet chocolate chips

1 tablespoon shortening

3/4 cup chopped walnuts

• In a large bowl, beat the eggs, oil and sugar. Stir in vanilla. Combine flour, cocoa and salt; gradually add to egg mixture. Stir in walnuts if desired.

• Pour into a greased 13-in. x 9-in. baking pan. Bake at 350° for 30 minutes or until brownies test done. Cool completely.

• For filling, in a large bowl, cream butter and sugars until light and fluffy. Beat in milk and vanilla. Gradually beat in flour. Spread over the brownies; chill until firm.

• For glaze, in a microwave, melt the chocolate chips and shortening; stir until smooth. Spread over filling. Immediately sprinkle with nuts, pressing down slightly.

YIELD: 36 SERVINGS.

coconut graham bars

PREP 20 min.

BAKE 15 min. + cooling

PATTY VAN ZYL • HOSPERS, IOWA

My mom calls these tempting morsels "Out of this World Bars." They go over well at any get-together.

2 cups graham cracker crumbs

1/2 cup sugar

1/2 cup butter, melted

2 cups flaked coconut

1 can (14 ounces) sweetened condensed milk

TOPPING:

1-1/2 cups packed brown sugar

6 tablespoons heavy whipping cream

1/4 cup butter, cubed

3/4 cup semisweet chocolate chips

• In a small bowl, combine the graham cracker crumbs, sugar and butter. Press onto the

CHEWY CHOCOLATE BROWNIES

bottom of a greased 13-in. x 9-in. baking pan. Bake at 350° for 8-10 minutes or until lightly browned.

• Combine the coconut and milk; spread over warm crust. Bake for 12-15 minutes or until the edges are lightly browned. Cool pan on a wire rack.

• In a large saucepan, combine the brown sugar, cream and butter. Bring to a boil over medium heat, stirring constantly. Boil for 1 minute. Remove from the heat; stir in chocolate chips until melted. Spread over coconut layer. Cool before cutting.

YIELD: 54 SERVINGS.

chewy chocolate brownies

PREP 15 min.

BAKE 15 min. + cooling

MICHELE DOUCETTE • STEPHENVILLE, NEWFOUNDLAND AND LABRADOR

These are so good, it's almost hard to believe that they're just 124 calories each!

3 ounces semisweet chocolate, chopped

1 cup packed brown sugar

3 tablespoons unsweetened applesauce

1 egg

1 egg white

2 tablespoons canola oil

4-1/2 teaspoons light corn syrup

2 teaspoons vanilla extract

1 cup all-purpose flour

1/4 cup baking cocoa

1/2 teaspoon baking soda

1/8 teaspoon salt

• In a microwave, melt chocolate; stir until smooth. Cool slightly. Meanwhile, in a large bowl, beat the brown sugar, applesauce, egg, egg white, oil, corn syrup and vanilla. Beat in chocolate until blended. Combine the flour, cocoa, baking soda and salt; beat into brown sugar mixture just until blended.

• Pour into a 13-in. x 9-in. baking pan coated with cooking spray. Bake at 350° for 15-18 minutes or until a toothpick inserted near the center comes out clean. Cool on a wire rack. Cut into bars.

YIELD: 18 SERVINGS.

cutting brownies and bars

To easily cut brownies or bars, line the baking pan with foil, leaving 3 inches hanging over each end. Grease the foil if recipe instructs. Once cool, use the foil to lift them out. Trim the edges of the treats and use a ruler to score the lines to cut. Use a serrated knife and cut downward.

chocolate-cherry cheesecake bars

PREP 20 min.

BAKE 20 min. + chilling

DARLENE BRENDEN • SALEM, OREGON

I've had this recipe longer than I can remember. I like to make these bars for Christmas, Valentine's Day or any occasion that calls for an extra-special treat.

- 1 cup all-purpose flour
- 1/2 cup packed brown sugar
- 1/3 cup cold butter, cubed
- 1/2 cup finely chopped walnuts
- 1 package (8 ounces) cream cheese, softened
- 1/2 cup sugar
- 1/3 cup baking cocoa
- 1 egg, lightly beaten
- 1/4 cup 2% milk
- 1/2 teaspoon vanilla extract
- 1/2 cup chopped maraschino cherries

Additional maraschino cherries, halved

- Place the flour, brown sugar and butter in a food processor; cover and process until fine crumbs form. Stir in walnuts. Set aside 3/4 cup for topping.

- Press remaining crumb mixture onto the bottom of an ungreased 8-in. square baking dish. Bake at 350° for 10 minutes or until set.

- Meanwhile, in a small bowl, beat the cream cheese, sugar and cocoa until smooth. Add the egg, milk and vanilla; beat on low speed just until combined. Stir in chopped cherries. Pour over crust; sprinkle with the reserved crumb mixture.

- Bake for 20-25 minutes or until center is almost set. Cool on a wire rack for 1 hour. Refrigerate for at least 2 hours.

- Cut into bars; top each with a cherry half. Store in the refrigerator.

YIELD: 15 SERVINGS.

cream cheese brownies

PREP 20 min.

BAKE 45 min. + chilling

BARBARA NITCZNSKI • DENVER, COLORADO

Brownies are a common dessert in our household because they're just about the only form of chocolate my husband will eat! I love this version, which makes a big batch and has a rich cream cheese layer in the center.

- 4 ounces unsweetened chocolate, chopped
- 1/2 cup butter, cubed
- 4 eggs
- 2 cups sugar
- 2 teaspoons vanilla extract
- 1-1/2 cups all-purpose flour
- 1 cup chopped nuts, optional

FILLING:

- 2 packages (8 ounces each) cream cheese, softened
- 1/2 cup sugar
- 1 egg
- 2 teaspoons vanilla extract

- In a microwave, melt chocolate and butter; stir until smooth. Cool slightly. In a large bowl, beat eggs and sugar. Stir in vanilla and chocolate mixture. Gradually add flour to chocolate mixture (batter will be thick). Stir in the nuts if desired.

- Spread half of the batter evenly in a greased 13-in. x 9-in. baking pan; set aside.

- In a small bowl, beat the filling ingredients until blended. Gently spread over the batter. Spoon the remaining batter over filling; spread to cover.

- Bake at 350° for 45-50 minutes or until filling is set. Cool on a wire rack for 1 hour.

- Refrigerate for at least 2 hours. Cut into bars. Refrigerate leftovers.

YIELD: 48 SERVINGS.

CHOCOLATE-CHERRY CHEESECAKE BARS

coconut brownies

PREP 15 min.

BAKE 25 min. + cooling

CAROL LIPP • TIMBER LAKE, SOUTH DAKOTA

My children and grandchildren are the light of my life. I always try to have homemade cookies or brownies on hand for them to nibble on when they visit. This recipe is one of their favorites.

- 1 cup butter, softened
- 2 cups sugar
- 4 eggs
- 1 teaspoon vanilla extract
- 1-1/2 cups all-purpose flour
- 1/2 cup plus 2 tablespoons baking cocoa
- 1/2 cup flaked coconut

- In a large bowl, cream butter and sugar until light and fluffy. Add eggs, one at a time, beating well after each addition. Beat in vanilla.

peanut butter brownies

PREP 15 min.
BAKE 30 min.

NICK WELTY • SMITHVILLE, OHIO

I like to prepare lots of pies, cakes, breads and bars to share at family gatherings and church potlucks. These chewy brownies are a big hit wherever I serve them.

- 3/4 cup shortening
- 3/4 cup peanut butter
- 2-1/4 cups sugar
- 5 eggs
- 1-1/2 teaspoons vanilla extract
- 1-1/2 cups all-purpose flour
- 1-1/2 teaspoons baking powder
- 3/4 teaspoon salt
- 1-1/2 cups semisweet chocolate chips
- 3/4 cup chopped peanuts

● In a large bowl, cream the shortening, peanut butter and sugar until light and fluffy. Beat in eggs and vanilla. Combine the flour, baking powder and salt; beat into creamed mixture just until blended. Stir in the chocolate chips and peanuts.

● Spread into a greased 15-in. x 10-in. x 1-in. baking pan. Bake at 350° for 30 minutes or until golden brown.

YIELD: 36 SERVINGS.

EDITOR'S NOTE: Reduced-fat or generic brands of peanut butter are not recommended for use in this recipe.

CHOCOLATE PEANUT SQUARES

Combine the flour and cocoa; gradually beat into creamed mixture just until blended. Stir in the coconut.

● Spread into a greased 13-in. x 9-in. baking pan. Bake at 350° for 22-25 minutes or until a toothpick inserted near the center comes out with moist crumbs (do not overbake). Cool on a wire rack.

YIELD: 18 SERVINGS.

chocolate peanut squares

PREP 15 min. + chilling

MARIE MARTIN • LITITZ, PENNSYLVANIA

I received this recipe from a friend at our local fire hall's annual quilting bee, where the ladies bring in goodies to serve at break time. It was a big hit with our family.

- 1 cup butter, *divided*
- 6 ounces semisweet chocolate, *divided*
- 1-1/2 cups graham cracker crumbs
- 1/2 cup unsalted dry roasted peanuts, chopped
- 2 packages (8 ounces *each*) cream cheese, softened
- 1 cup sugar
- 1 teaspoon vanilla extract

● In a small microwave-safe bowl, melt 3/4 cup butter and two ounces of chocolate; stir until smooth. Stir in cracker crumbs and peanuts.

● Press into a greased 13-in. x 9-in. pan. Cover and refrigerate for 30 minutes or until set.

● In a small bowl, beat the cream cheese, sugar and vanilla until fluffy. Spread over chocolate layer.

● Melt the remaining butter and chocolate; stir until smooth. Carefully spread over cream cheese layer. Cover and refrigerate until set. Cut into squares.

YIELD: 24 SERVINGS.

tip

a fancy touch

Dress up brownies or blondies by placing them on individual serving plates drizzled with chocolate syrup. Top each with a scoop of chocolate or vanilla ice cream, then add some more chocolate syrup, a spoonful of whipped cream and a maraschino cherry for the crowning touch.

PEANUT BUTTER BROWNIES

diamond almond bars

PREP 20 min.
BAKE 25 min. + cooling

LIZ GREEN • TAMWORTH, ONTARIO

Making these chewy almond bar cookies has been a tradition in our family for generations. They're especially popular at holiday time. I always freeze several dozen to enjoy into the New Year.

- 1 cup butter, softened
- 1 cup plus 1 tablespoon sugar, *divided*
- 1 egg, *separated*
- 1 teaspoon almond extract
- 2 cups all-purpose flour
- 1/2 cup blanched sliced almonds
- 1/4 teaspoon ground cinnamon

• In a large bowl, cream butter and 1 cup sugar until light and fluffy. Add egg yolk; beat well. Stir in extract. Add flour, beating until combined.

• Press into a greased 15-in. x 10-in. x 1-in. baking pan. Beat egg white until foamy; brush over dough. Top with almonds. Combine the cinnamon and remaining sugar; sprinkle over the top.

• Bake at 350° for 25-30 minutes or until lightly browned (do not overbake). Cool on a wire rack for 10 minutes. Cut into diamond-shaped bars. Cool completely.

YIELD: 60 SERVINGS.

FUDGE-NUT OATMEAL BARS

DIAMOND ALMOND BARS

fudge-nut oatmeal bars

PREP 20 min.
BAKE 20 min.

KIM STOLLER • SMITHVILLE, OHIO

These heavenly bars always seem to disappear in a jiffy!

- 1 cup butter, softened
- 2 cups packed brown sugar
- 2 eggs
- 2 teaspoons vanilla extract
- 3 cups quick-cooking oats
- 2-1/2 cups all-purpose flour
- 1 teaspoon baking soda
- 1 teaspoon salt

FUDGE FILLING

- 1 can (14 ounces) sweetened condensed milk
- 2 cups (12 ounces) semisweet chocolate chips
- 2 tablespoons butter
- 1/2 teaspoon salt
- 1 cup chopped walnuts
- 2 teaspoons vanilla extract

• In a bowl, cream butter and brown sugar until light and fluffy. Add eggs and vanilla; mix well. Combine oats, flour, baking soda and salt; add to the creamed mixture. Spread two-thirds into an ungreased 15-in. x 10-in. x 1-in. baking pan; set aside.

• For the filling, heat the milk, chocolate chips, butter and salt in a microwave-safe bowl until chips are melted. Remove from the heat; stir in walnuts and vanilla. Spread over top. Drop the remaining oat mixture by tablespoonfuls over chocolate.

• Bake at 350° for 20 to 25 minutes. Cool on a wire rack.

YIELD: 30 SERVINGS.

storing brownies and bars

Cover a pan of uncut brownies or bars with foil. (If made with perishable ingredients, like cream cheese, store covered in the refrigerator.) Once cut, store them in an airtight container. Most bars and brownies freeze well for up to 3 months.

no-bake bars

PREP 20 min.

SUSIE WINGERT • PANAMA, IOWA

This dessert is big on taste but takes only a little effort. It's especially handy to make when the weather is hot, since the oven never has to be turned on.

- 4 cups Cheerios
- 2 cups crisp rice cereal
- 2 cups dry roasted peanuts
- 2 cups M&M's
- 1 cup light corn syrup
- 1 cup sugar
- 1-1/2 cups creamy peanut butter
- 1 teaspoon vanilla extract

● In a large bowl, combine the first four ingredients; set aside. In a large saucepan, bring corn syrup and sugar to a boil. Cook and stir just until sugar is dissolved.

● Remove from the heat; stir in peanut butter and vanilla. Pour over cereal mixture; toss to coat evenly. Spread into a greased 15-in. x 10-in. x 1-in. pan. Cool. Cut into 3-in. squares.

YIELD: 15 SERVINGS.

applesauce brownies

PREP 15 min.

BAKE 25 min. + cooling

BERNICE PEBLEY • COZAD, NEBRASKA

These moist, cinnamon-flavored brownies are quite easy to make. The recipe can also be doubled and baked in a jelly roll pan.

- 1/4 cup butter
- 3/4 cup sugar
- 1 egg
- 1 cup all-purpose flour
- 1 tablespoon baking cocoa
- 1/2 teaspoon baking soda
- 1/2 teaspoon ground cinnamon
- 1 cup applesauce

TOPPING:

- 1/2 cup chocolate chips
- 1/2 cup chopped walnuts *or* pecans
- 1 tablespoon sugar

● In a large bowl, cream butter and sugar until light and fluffy. Beat in egg. Combine the flour, cocoa, baking soda and cinnamon; gradually add to creamed mixture and mix well. Stir in applesauce. Pour into a greased 8-in. square baking pan.

● Combine topping ingredients; sprinkle over batter. Bake at 350° for 25 minutes or until toothpick inserted near the center comes out clean. Cool before cutting into squares.

YIELD: 16 SERVINGS.

white chocolate cranberry blondies

PREP 35 min.

BAKE 20 min. + cooling

ERIKA BUSZ • KENT, WASHINGTON

These blondies are requested often at our house. For a more fancy presentation, cut the bars into triangles and then drizzle white chocolate over each one.

- 3/4 cup butter, cubed
- 1-1/2 cups packed light brown sugar
- 2 eggs
- 3/4 teaspoon vanilla extract
- 2-1/4 cups all-purpose flour
- 1-1/2 teaspoons baking powder
- 1/4 teaspoon salt
- 1/8 teaspoon ground cinnamon
- 1/2 cup dried cranberries
- 6 ounces white baking chocolate, coarsely chopped

FROSTING:

- 1 package (8 ounces) cream cheese, softened
- 1 cup confectioners' sugar
- 1 tablespoon grated orange peel, optional
- 6 ounces white baking chocolate, melted
- 1/2 cup dried cranberries, chopped

● In a microwave, melt butter; stir in brown sugar. Transfer to a large bowl; cool to room temperature. Beat in the eggs and vanilla. Combine the flour, baking powder, salt and cinnamon; gradually add to butter mixture. Stir in cranberries and chopped chocolate (batter will be thick).

● Spread into a greased 13-in. x 9-in. baking dish. Bake at 350° for 18-21 minutes or until a toothpick inserted near the center comes out clean (do not overbake). Cool on a wire rack.

● For frosting, in a large bowl, beat the cream cheese, confectioners' sugar and orange peel if desired until blended. Gradually add half of the melted white chocolate; beat until blended. Frost brownies. Sprinkle with cranberries. Drizzle with remaining melted white chocolate. Cut into bars. Store in the refrigerator.

YIELD: 30 SERVINGS.

WHITE CHOCOLATE CRANBERRY BLONDIES

APRICOT BARS

apricot bars

PREP 25 min.
BAKE 25 min. + cooling

BARBARA ROHLF • SPIRIT LAKE, IOWA

I've had so many favorable comments from folks who sample this cookie-like creation. The sweet apricot flavor and sprinkling of coconut make these bars extra-special!

- 1 package (16 ounces) pound cake mix
- 4 eggs
- 1/2 cup butter, melted
- 2 teaspoons vanilla extract, *divided*
- 1 cup chopped dried apricots
- 1 package (8 ounces) cream cheese, softened
- 2 cups confectioners' sugar
- 1/2 cup apricot preserves
- 3/4 cup flaked coconut
- 3/4 cup sliced almonds

● In a large bowl, combine the cake mix, 2 eggs, butter and 1 teaspoon vanilla; beat until well blended. Fold in the dried apricots. Spread into a greased 15-in. x 10-in. x 1-in. baking pan; set aside.

● In another bowl, beat the cream cheese, confectioners' sugar, preserves and remaining vanilla. Add the remaining eggs; beat on low speed just until combined. Gently spread over cake batter. Sprinkle with the coconut and almonds.

● Bake at 350° for 25-30 minutes or until golden brown. Cool on a wire rack. Cut into bars. Refrigerate leftovers.

YIELD: 24 SERVINGS.

peanut butter cake bars

PREP 15 min.
BAKE 45 min. + cooling

CHARLOTTE ENNIS
LAKE ARTHUR, NEW MEXICO

These cake-like treats are packed with peanut butter and chocolate chips, and are perfect for any occasion. Kids and adults alike are in for a treat when you serve them.

- 2/3 cup butter, softened
- 2/3 cup peanut butter
- 1 cup sugar
- 1 cup packed brown sugar
- 4 eggs
- 2 teaspoons vanilla extract
- 2 cups all-purpose flour
- 2 teaspoons baking powder
- 1/2 teaspoon salt
- 1 package (11-1/2 ounces) milk chocolate chips

● In a large bowl, cream the butter, peanut butter, sugar and brown sugar. Add eggs, one at a time, beating well after each addition. Beat in vanilla. Combine the flour, baking powder and salt; gradually add to creamed mixture. Stir in chocolate chips.

● Spread into a greased 13-in. x 9-in. baking pan. Bake at 350° for 45-50 minutes or until a toothpick inserted near the center comes out clean. Cool on a wire rack. Cut into bars.

YIELD: 24 SERVINGS.

rich butterscotch bars

PREP 15 min.
BAKE 30 min. + cooling

KATHRYN ROTH • JEFFERSON, WISCONSIN

My husband works second shift, so I spend a few nights a week baking just for fun. He takes half of my sweets to his coworkers, who frequently ask for these tasty bars.

- 1 package (10 to 11 ounces) butterscotch chips
- 1/2 cup butter, cubed
- 2 cups graham cracker crumbs (about 32 squares)
- 1 package (8 ounces) cream cheese, softened
- 1 can (14 ounces) sweetened condensed milk
- 1 egg
- 1 teaspoon vanilla extract
- 1 cup chopped pecans

● In a microwave, melt chips and butter; stir until smooth. Add cracker crumbs; set aside 2/3 cup. Press the remaining crumb mixture into a greased 13-in. x 9-in. baking pan.

● In a small bowl, beat cream cheese until smooth. Beat in the milk, egg and vanilla. Stir in pecans.

● Pour over the crust. Sprinkle with reserved crumb mixture. Bake at 325° for 30-35 minutes or until a toothpick inserted near the center comes out clean. Cool on a wire rack. Store in the refrigerator.

YIELD: 36 SERVINGS.

chocolate strawberry truffle brownies

PREP 30 min.
BAKE 30 min. + chilling

TERESA JANSEN • ADVANCE, MISSOURI

Every summer I make strawberry jam, and one day I decided to add some to a batch of brownies. They were a hit with my family. I also like to treat the students in all of my special ed classes to these delectable treats.

1-1/4 cups semisweet chocolate chips
1/2 cup butter, cubed
3/4 cup packed brown sugar
2 eggs
1 teaspoon instant coffee granules
2 tablespoons water
3/4 cup all-purpose flour
1/2 teaspoon baking powder

TRUFFLE FILLING:

1 cup (6 ounces) semisweet chocolate chips
1/4 teaspoon instant coffee granules
1 package (8 ounces) cream cheese, softened
1/4 cup sifted confectioners' sugar
1/3 cup strawberry jam or preserves

GLAZE:

1/4 cup semisweet chocolate chips
1 teaspoon shortening

- In a microwave, melt chocolate and butter; stir until smooth. Cool slightly. In a large bowl, beat brown sugar and eggs. Stir in chocolate mixture. Dissolve coffee in water; add to chocolate mixture. Combine flour and baking powder; gradually add to batter.

- Spread evenly in a greased and floured 9-in. square baking pan. Bake at 350° for 30-35 minutes or until a toothpick inserted near the center comes out clean. Cool.

- Meanwhile, for filling, melt the chocolate chips and coffee granules; stir until smooth. Set aside.

- In a small bowl, beat the cream cheese until smooth. Add confectioners' sugar and jam; mix well. Beat in melted chocolate until well blended. Spread over brownies.

- For glaze, in a microwave, melt chocolate and shortening; stir until smooth. Drizzle over filling. Chill at least 1-2 hours.

YIELD: 24 SERVINGS.

RASPBERRY PATCH CRUMB BARS

raspberry patch crumb bars

PREP 30 min.
BAKE 35 min. + cooling

LEANNA THORNE • LAKEWOOD, COLORADO

To give these fruity bars even more crunch, add a sprinkling of nuts to the melt-in-your-mouth topping. Everyone will want to indulge.

3 cups all-purpose flour
1-1/2 cups sugar, *divided*
1 teaspoon baking powder
1/4 teaspoon salt
1/4 teaspoon ground cinnamon
1 cup shortening
2 eggs, lightly beaten
1 teaspoon almond extract
1 tablespoon cornstarch
4 cups fresh or frozen raspberries

- In a large bowl, combine the flour, 1 cup sugar, baking powder, salt and cinnamon. Cut in shortening until mixture resembles coarse crumbs. Stir in eggs and extract. Press two-thirds of the mixture into a greased 13-in. x 9-in. baking dish.

- In a large bowl, combine the cornstarch and remaining sugar; add berries and gently toss. Spoon over crust. Sprinkle with the remaining crumb mixture.

- Bake at 375° for 35-45 minutes or until bubbly and golden brown. Cool on a wire rack. Cut into bars. Store in the refrigerator.

YIELD: 36 SERVINGS.

EDITOR'S NOTE: If using frozen raspberries, do not thaw before tossing them with the cornstarch mixture.

CHOCOLATE STRAWBERRY TRUFFLE BROWNIES

general recipe index

This index lists every recipe by food category and/or major ingredient, so you can easily locate recipes to suit your needs.

alphabetical index

This index lists every recipe in alphabetical order
so you can easily find your favorite recipes.